Saving Remnants

Dianne Threatt Evans

A publication of

Eber & Wein Publishing

Pennsylvania

Library of Congress
Cataloging in Publication Data

ISBN 978-1-60880-672-0

Proudly manufactured in the United States of America by

Eber & Wein Publishing
Pennsylvania

DEDICATION

"... Hold fast to dreams,
For when dreams die,
Life becomes a broken-winged bird
That cannot fly."

—Langston Hughes

I am opening my box of remnants to pay homage to the melancholy children who are enclosed there: those who are misplaced, mistreated, or misunderstood. Those who cannot fly.

It is dedicated to all caregivers in schools, agencies, clinics, hospitals, and home-care facilities who seek—however futile their efforts may be—to give flight to those bruised and battered wings.

It is especially honoring my own spirited children, Dawn and Dana, who through their sweeping celebration of life, have helped their mother hold fast to dreams.

It is for their father, my husband, Donnie, who gives me hope and renewed wings.

It is for Evan Williamson, Samuel Alexander, and Ellison Edward McDow, my grandsons, who cover me in the enraptured abundance of cherished, joyful memories.

It is for my mama.

CONTENTS

PREFACE

As a child, I would often go into the den closet and rummage through the box of cloth scraps my mother was saving there. She, being a talented and skilled seamstress, would save remnants of cloth from numerous garments she had designed and made. I loved to feel the sleekness of the silks, or the softness of the velvet, and the crispness of the organdy and lace. But even more so, I loved to remember the sundresses, or the draperies, or the recital gowns. These scraps of cloth were remnants of spent days. From these many different fabrics of various sizes and shapes, she would make beautiful, cozy quilts that would cover us all in memories.

We all save our remnants—reminders of spent days. Perhaps it is in pictures placed in photo albums or on computer screens and smart phones, or souvenirs and mementos tucked safely away in a trunk or cabinet. I, too, have those, but my visual memory—lingering always—seems to serve me best.

I offer you my box of remnants in book form. In this book, you will find children of various sizes and shapes. I have saved remnants of these children in the closet of my mind for almost half a century while I served as a teacher, counselor, and school psychologist.

Open it carefully. Find the softness of the worn fabrics; search for the beauty in the torn pieces. See the potential each remnant holds to become more than a discarded scrap.

**"Somewhere children dance to the joyous music of life
and elsewhere they only cling to existence.
They are all ours."**

—Laurie Kohl

INTRODUCTION

I was a young woman, armed with idealism and compassion, awaiting my first group of emotionally-disturbed and socially-maladjusted children in a public school setting. They came to me—this curious bunch of fragmented children—displaying, through peculiar manifestations, behaviors that spoke vividly of that which they could neither articulate nor understand. I saw unidentified needs and unspoken fears taking flight on broken wings destined only to falter. It was my task to teach them how to cope with themselves and to adjust to a world that cared not to embrace them.

Through years of my own classroom experiences, through observations and evaluations of other classrooms housing similar children, I have emerged. I am no longer a young woman. My idealism has diminished; my compassion deepened. Both have been tempered with objectivity, and both have been embellished with hope.

A child, damaged though he or she may be, is still a wondrous and resilient creature from whom we can learn much. By sharing fragments of these children's plights, it is my perpetual hope that such children everywhere may be met with compassion and afforded a chance to fly.

Each remnant I offer you is a true representation of the child from whom it came. The conversations, too, are authentic. Only names have been changed.

Saving Remnants

I. The Beckoning

"Know well the condition of your flocks, and give attention to your herds."

—Proverbs 27:23 (RSV)

JOHN'S SILENT SOUND

On a bleak school day in October, I noticed on the daily absentee bulletin that John and two other boys had been suspended from school for three days.

John had been in my homeroom section two years earlier when I was teaching general education classes. Spending ten minutes daily to check attendance, take up lunch money, and other menial tasks, I noticed that he was always on time. He was always seated and never spoke except to answer when his name was called. Thinking back, I see him now as he sat still and placid, showing little emotion. He usually looked out the window or rested his head, face down, into his crossed arms. This had been my only contact with him—ten minutes each day—two years ago when he was in attendance.

He didn't seem a likely person to be suspended from school. When I inquired as to why he had been suspended, I learned that he, along with the other boys, had cut class without permission, without reason as it seemed. They were taken out of school for three days because they had missed one class one day.

It takes a lot of dedicated time and creative energy to plan and implement effective and individualized punishment for every offense committed in a typical school day.

Would that we should try.

It was late afternoon of the following day before the sun shone through the bleakness. Even so, its brightness could not lift the gray stillness that had settled upon us.

At some unknown time during those two days, John walked into the woods near his home and found a resting place near a stream. There, with his only companion—a sawed-off shotgun—he ended his fifteen years of living.

There were those in our school community who repeatedly asked, "Why?"

Superficial conclusions followed; shallow explanations were offered, such as:

"He hated school; he was failing every class."

"He was afraid to tell his father that he had been suspended."

None sufficed.

If we would take the painful opportunity to investigate with great patience and persistence all the circumstances, internal and external, connected with his suicide, I believe we would find a very different basis for its etiology.

What we must remember is that persons who commit suicide have self-destructive tendencies that are internal long before the external precipitating circumstances occur, such as suspension from school. We must remember, too, that all deeply-depressed people are potential suicides. And most important of all, some apparently seem to be "normal persons."

However, it is up to us who pass as "normal" to be vigilant enough to recognize disturbances that hinder personal development in all of life's children, whatever their age. Most importantly, we must recognize that suicide is never the first symptom of the mental state it terminates.

We, the trained, caring professionals in this public education system, must have not remembered. We must have been too busy taking up lunch money and calling the roll, or administering meaningless punishment. Time spent with a child who is creating no disturbance, who speaks only when spoken to, is time that could be spent hushing the obscene or attending to the slow.

It is difficult to hear those silent disturbances that hinder personal development when one is not listening. It takes a lot of time and creative energy to speak to every estrangement that might occur in a typical school day when one is engrossed in other tasks.

Would that we should try.

The devastating sadness of it all is that it is too late for John. I had him for ten minutes each day he was in attendance two years earlier. The fact that many other people had more time and opportunity is of little comfort to me.

This event was a great impetus that compelled me to go back to college and earn two graduate degrees in school psychology. After that, I began my work with exceptional children—those outside the norm.

**"The reality of the other person
is not in what he reveals to you,
but in what he cannot reveal to you.
Therefore, if you would understand him,
listen not to what he says,
but rather to what he does not say."**

—Kahlil Gibran, *Sand and Foam*

The Beckoning Continues:

Of what value am I? . . .
"A broken-winged bird that cannot fly . . ."

MELISSA'S SECRET

Old and weary was this child. Large and matronly, she walked slowly and without spirit. There was, seemingly, no music to dance to in her soul. She, a quiet, somber sixteen-year-old, presenting no problem to anyone, required little attention from faculty or staff. Yet she, like many others who are not identified as disturbed, was, nevertheless, suffering quietly, screaming silently, plodding through adolescence wearily without progress. This is Melissa's story:

She comes to me—her teacher—to share a long-kept secret.

I listen to her expressionless voice uncovering the rehearsed words carefully. Eyes that had been purged of brightness looked beyond me into a place where she knows I cannot go. As if she were describing someone other than herself, she tells me of the nights her father forced her to have sexual intercourse with him since she was ten years old.

As she laboriously tells her agonizing secret, her torment seems to lessen. She knows she will be released, by her telling, from a victimization that she can no longer bear. She knows, too, by her own admission, that more suffering will surely follow. She is ready now, she says, to end her captivity regardless of the unknown consequences. As she untangles the control that misshaped her, her eyes retreat to my face, searching for affirmation.

She finds it there.

She thanks me for listening, for understanding, for my pledge to begin the forces that would end this six-year misery and initiate the healing process. But it is I who should thank her.

It is I who am humbled and inspired by the courage of this weary child who takes a stand against the morass of confusion that has so long bound her. She has crossed the abyss of shame and fear and she and I both will emerge—by her sharing—stronger.

When I am face-to-face with a child who is heavy with sorrow, one who has been painfully robbed of the right to be a child, and that same child still believes there is hope for a better future, I am always struck with a feeling of reverence. It is I who should thank these children for allowing me to see such faith. Somehow, they still believe there is enough good in the world that someone will care—someone will help—someone will offer a place of solace.

It is such faith, such worth, such courage that enables me, not only to believe it, too, but to act upon it with the same abiding force.

"When the satisfaction, security, and development of another person become as significant to you as your own satisfaction, security, and development, love exists."

—Harry Stack Sullivan

II. THE MOBILE UNIT

". . . You have scattered my flock, and have driven them away, and have not attended to them . . . I will gather the remnant of my flock . . . and I will bring them back to their fold . . ."

—Jeremiah 23:2-3 (RSV)

As schools ran out of adequate space to house the number of students enrolled, mobile units were brought to the campuses to provide additional sites to hold classes.

I was assigned to a mobile unit, which was situated behind the main school building. That suited me fine. It gave the students I was serving an opportunity to leave the main school building and take a brief walk outside to the mobile unit. Once inside, it served us well as an entity apart from—yet belonging to—the rest of the school. That's exactly what we were:

AN ENTITY APART

The moment of entry into the mobile unit is always pleasant to me. The green carpet holds a hint of yellow intermingled with slices of bright orange—as well as traces of yesterday's footprints. The bright yellow-and-orange checked curtains, made by my mother, adorn the four windows. The worn, upholstered brown sofa and green chair with matching ottoman, discarded from my Aunt Ola's house, are invitations inside the homey spaciousness.

Colorful posters send messages from the wall to children encouraging them to try; to believe; and, yes, to laugh. My favorite among the pictures, books, and funny little statues donated to the mobile unit from students long since gone is a decoupage plaque made by Susan, which holds a sprig of grass beside the words:

"Upon those who love, ungenerous time bestows a thousand summers."

Susan is at the university now aspiring to have some summers she missed.

As the door is opened, the first thing visible is eleven desks circled together on the right side of the room. This is where the students must sit as they tackle academic tasks. Across the floor to the left, the old furniture sits. It is here that we hold discussions, tell stories, and listen to students' concerns. Except for the eleven desks circled together on one side of the mobile unit, it looks little like a classroom. It *is* little like a classroom. It is a psycho-educational resource program serving emotionally-disturbed children.

Once I enter, I must be one-hundred-percent available to meet the children and youth who are referred to me. This includes those who are suffering from mild, transitory problems to those who have severe, deep-rooted conflicts. All have academic problems. I cannot be half ready to meet them, nor can I be unprepared in daily plans or long-range goals. Often though, daily plans are put aside when life demands another task for the day. Yet in everything we do, there must be a thrust forward.

When you are a fourteen-year-old pregnant girl who has been deserted by your older boyfriend, it is hard to really care about subject and verb agreements. When you are a twelve-year-old boy who has run away from home for the third time with the choice of going back to a prostitute mother or to a detention center, finding the unknown in a math equation is not nearly as important as trying to piece together shattered segments of your life.

While I attempt to teach effective coping skills and the beginning of self-understanding to students with various types of problems, it is extremely important that I separate my needs from theirs. Within myself, I must claim responsibility for recognizing and dealing with my own needs, my own biases, my own prejudices, or preconceptions. I cannot allow such as this to interfere or cloud my ability to meet the developmental needs of my students.

How important it is for me to be well-integrated when Glenn, an aggressive and angry teen (for so many unfortunate reasons), says to me, "I've been coming out here for a year and I ain't never learned nothin'."

Sure, it hurt. But I cannot (nor can he) deal with my need to be a "good teacher" at that moment. I have to lay aside that need and hear what he may be saying underneath the noise he's making.

"I'm going back to my old ways," he threatened. "I'm going to get high and forget this whole damn school mess."

The choice is ultimately his. I cannot make it for him. This attitude of, "If you won't do it for yourself, then do it for me," is sometimes used by parents and teachers. And, indeed, it does work at times.

But greater risk is involved if the child fails and he also feels that he has failed a significant person in his life. This added defeat can lead to more disaster. On the other hand, if the child succeeds, he will not feel the need to give the credit of his success to one other than himself.

The magic comes if—in the presentation of alternatives and new reward systems—I somehow succeed in guiding them to some new values and new behaviors.

It is a painful, slow journey to the honest path of self-examination. The individual must realize a need for change before change can occur. That change must be identified and strategies developed that will make the learning process successful. These children—no different from us—are ready to work only when their present defenses fail to work for them.

My mind will always hold within it the picture of children in distress trying to grow into a tomorrow that must be better. My heart will always feel their panic and know their disillusionment. And yet, there has to be some degree of objectivity in order to serve them well. Perhaps that is the real magic—this merging of empathy and objectivity. It is extremely hard to do.

Sometimes, I think it is an impossible task I have before me. But, I have yet to give up. Like the Lady of the Harbor, I see *"the tired, the poor, the huddled masses yearning to be free . . . ."* And, like her, I wonder if I, too, have over-extended my boundaries.

"This is the true joy in life, the being used for a purpose recognized by yourself as a mighty one."

—George Bernard Shaw

SADIE

Big and brawny,
Bad and brown,
Eighth-grade "super cool."

With plowman-like stride
And gutter slang,
She had everybody fooled.

Yeah, she smoked a little pot,
Drank a little booze,
Even turned a trick or two.

But she cried alone
A lot at night.
She didn't have Sadie fooled.

She liked raccoons
And kitty-cats,
And if the truth were told:
She made a rag bed,
Saved crumbs, and fed
The mice that scampered 'round her head
In this place
She never said
                    she wanted to call home.

Sadie was "King of the Hill." To describe her as queen would not suffice; she was definitely "King." She worked on this image constantly. It was seemingly her one aspiration in life—to remain the biggest and baddest in eighth grade.

Being two grade levels behind her age group she had little prospective rivals and she proudly knew it. Her size, coupled with her loud, abusive talk convinced those who would challenge her that this moose-of-a-girl was too tough to tackle.

Only occasionally had I managed to get her down from her frenzies to tune in to other aspects of herself. She could—in rare, quiet moments of feeling—write vivid poetry.

"I am like the wind," she had written. "I fly unknown around the world looking for a place to be."

Yet, she fought me and herself against those times that required her to think. To touch her inner self was risky. To be gentle was to be vulnerable.

The unknown segment of her that screamed frantically to be loved and lovely could be heard only if someone put forth the unyielding persistence to listen. And that was not easy to do.

Who wanted to listen to Sadie's inner voice? "Ha," I heard some jeer. "That obnoxious girl; she's crazy. It'll be a good day for this school when she drops out." And, of course, the inevitable came.

They had not seen her—guided by trust in my words—restrain herself enough to keep her voice down and her guard down. She lowered her aggressive defense and even tried to be more lady-like when he was near. He was, at that time, her other aspiration in life. Perhaps it was futile, but she so wanted him to like her.

She had even donned a dress—rather than her usual unattractive garb—on the day she knew he was coming. I watched her in the classroom setting of our mobile unit as she moved her chair closer to him and smiled.

His laughter at her efforts to appeal was brutal. "Soft and sexy, Sadie," he sneered. "I can't believe this. Get away from me, you crazy girl," he said as he pushed at her chair.

"Yeah, and I'll beat your damn ass," she yelled as she jumped up in retaliation, fighting bravely against the loss that could engulf her.

This he could believe. He did not challenge her, but walked away laughing at the "King of the Hill."

Less than two hours later, during my lunch break, I was summoned to the principal's office.

Oh, God, I thought as I rushed down the hall. *What is it this time?*

Mr. Graves, the principal, opened the door to reveal a flush-faced Sadie.

"Mrs. Evans," the principal began, "I just wanted to let you know that I have suspended Sadie for three days for fighting. That's the rule: Fighting on school grounds is an immediate suspension. It's in the student handbook. Have you gone over the handbook with these students?" he asked.

"Yes," I replied. "What happened, Sadie?" I asked her.

Mr. Graves did not give her time to answer. "She just jumped Jamie Stokes at his locker; she hit him in the head with her book-bag, causing him to fall to the floor. This could have resulted in a serious injury."

"He was laughing at me, Mrs. Evans," a tear-eyed Sadie tried to explain. "He was telling all the kids around that I had tried to hook up with him this morning in the mobile unit, and they were all laughing."

I nodded my head.

"Go straight to detention hall until the end of the school day," Mr. Graves ordered.

When she had left, I turned to Mr. Graves and said, "You can't suspend her. There is a federal law (Public Law 94-142) that prevents suspending students due to their handicapping condition. She has been diagnosed as emotionally-disturbed. That is her handicapping condition; her behavior is due to her emotional disturbance, so suspending her is out of the question. We certainly don't want to lose federal funding over this, do we?"

"She is not emotionally-disturbed, Mrs. Evans," he said curtly. "She's just mean as hell. The suspension stands."

"Being mean as hell," I said—softer and slower now— "especially when it's a child is indicative of emotional disturbance."

"The suspension stands, Mrs. Evans," he said with obvious dismissal in his tone.

I had lost my lunch time and my argument.

Sadie had been retained for two years in first grade and for two years in third grade. It would not be long now before she would be old enough to drop out of school. Her compulsory school attendance would end at her next birthday.

After that day of suspension, Sadie never returned to school. I have never seen her since that day. I often think of Sadie.

Big Sadie, soft and sad; is she still like the wind? Is she still rushing wildly among us looking for a place to be?

"There is no greater curse than discontent . . ."
—Lao-tsu

Marcus & Shellie

Marcus and Shellie, two seventh-grade boys who were the best of friends, are sweet remnants stored in the attic of my mind, or perhaps, in the depths of my heart. They, and four other seventh and eighth grade boys, were scheduled into my second-period class. I do not know if their friendship arose from their being together in my resource room for the emotionally and socially impaired, or if they were friends before entering my program. Whichever the case, I do believe that their friendship was borne out of desperation. They came together because of their lack of peer approval—no one else would befriend them.

Emotionally-disturbed children do not make friends easily. Part of this is due to some unusual behaviors that they may manifest, which turn others away. Some may appear too needy and clingy; others, too bossy and aggressive. Such behaviors can scatter would-be friends asunder. Or, it may be the fact that they are just distant and unapproachable—as is Marcus—whose primary behavior is withdrawal.

Marcus is a tub. Less than five feet tall, he appears to be round like a pumpkin from his neck down to his thighs. He plods along lethargically, lifting each foot as if it were a heavy burden. This only calls attention to those tiny, little feet, which seem much too small to carry around such weight. He enters the room slowly, moving his body from side to side with each step he takes. He goes directly to his chair.

I have placed a straight-back chair slightly apart from the others' circle with a regular student desk turned sideways in front of it. This is done so that he will have a flat surface on which to complete his work. His middle body is too large to fit into a regular school desk. No matter where I put his chair and desk, he will always push them farther away from the others' circle. He will sit there in an almost catatonic state during the entire hour of class if I let him.

To engage Marcus in a task, I often must go to him and cup both my hands on his face, turn it toward me, and speak to him in an above-normal tone to bring him out of the silent abyss in which he chooses to dwell. But once engaged, he will complete the assignment quickly so he can return to his state of withdrawal.

His level of intelligence (scores obtained from the WISC-R) puts him in the high average range, and he is much smarter than the other five children in his class. He can easily do what is required of him academically. Except for his constant withdrawal, there is no other disturbing factor from Marcus.

The most distinguishing aspect of Marcus—other than his size—is that he is always clean and neatly-dressed. This communicates to me that someone at home does care about him. I notice this particularly because the children I serve are often not clean and well-groomed. Such is the case with Shellie.

Shellie (whose birth name is Sheldon) is a very skinny and disheveled-looking little boy. He comes in the room with Marcus, but in a very different manner. He enters as if blown in by a strong wind. He does not sit; he walks around the room chattering to himself until he approaches me.

"Look at my new shoes, Mrs. Evans," he says as he picks up one foot for me to see. The shoes are brown and white men's dress shoes and they are too big for his feet. "My mama got them at a garage sale for only fifty cents," he proudly reports.

Jacob, who is always ready to heap criticism on others, is about to laugh at Shellie's shoes. I can see the smirk on his face that speaks before he does. I raise a finger and shake my head from side-to-side so as to abort his cruel words. In this class of six boys, so many different behaviors abound—some threatening to others; some helpful to others. It is I, the teacher, who must be vigilant enough to decide which is which and recognize the possible consequences of all behaviors exhibited.

Shellie has been diagnosed with ADHD (attention-deficit/hyperactivity disorder). As hard as it is to get Marcus engaged, it is equally as difficult to get Shellie still enough to attend to an assigned task. ADHD describes an array of symptoms that include excessive inattention, overactivity, and impulsivity. Shellie displays all of these behaviors. He does not, however, show hostility and aggression. Many children with ADHD have conduct disorder as well.

Children with conduct disorder are much more non-compliant and harder to manage. Shellie is hard to manage, but he has a happy demeanor and I find him to be a rather endearing child, despite his perpetual movement and silly outbursts.

The two primary methods of intervention for ADHD are stimulant medication and behavioral management. Shellie says, "Sometimes I take my medicine and sometimes I don't." I rely on behavior management techniques because I do not administer his medication. I am also trying to teach him impulse control because I do not want him to rely solely on medicine for self-management.

On-task behavior and compliance to teacher requests are important ways to earn much sought-after tokens in the behavior modification program I operate in this classroom. Earned tokens can be cashed in at the end of each week for rewards. The underlying lesson, of course, is to teach children that they are responsible for their own behaviors, and that only certain behaviors are appropriate for positive reinforcement. Tokens (brightly-colored, round, plastic disks) are collected in small jars on their desks. Tokens are administered by me. I drop tokens into the slit in the top of the jar as they are earned.

Shellie does not stay on task. He often talks while others are working; he gets up and down; he clowns around. Offering up such distractions will cost him the few tokens he may have earned from appropriate behaviors. Response cost is the term used to describe inappropriate behaviors that cause students to lose tokens. Students are well aware of the consequences of their behavior. I gave them the opportunity to help devise the menu of appropriate and inappropriate behaviors. I did this partly so they would be met with no surprises. Also, if they had input, they would be more likely to accept the standards imposed. They know the actions that will bring about the positive reinforcement of earned tokens, and those actions that will take those tokens away.

It is the end of the week and students eagerly anticipate re-deeming their tokens. Each student is allowed to empty his jar and count the earned tokens. All rewards available are clearly marked with the "price" needed to acquire them. Some rewards are edible (candy, fruit, etc.). Other rewards include free time at the math computer, puzzle games, building model airplanes, cars, or Lego creations. (Once started, completions of these structures will require more earned tokens due to the time involved and the time allowed during each class period.) I also have some gift certificates that can be used at different fast-food restaurants.

Yes, there are educational experts who profess that external rewards such as these do not teach self-discipline. They predict that when the rewards are no longer forthcoming, previous behaviors will resurface. Yet, I have found that tokens work well when I also provide positive feedback, praise, smiles, and other forms of verbal and non-verbal rewards for progress. Praising and rewarding on-task and prosocial behaviors while gradually requiring more from the students helps them develop persistence for meeting higher standards. By-products of this process include courtesy and character-building as well as the ability to accept the delay of gratification (I hope).

Marcus has more tokens than anyone in the class because he does not manifest any problematic behaviors except withdrawal. He is proud of this and chooses free time on the problem-solving math computer game, which is a high-cost item.

Shellie has no tokens. The few he has earned he had to pay back due to behaviors that are not acceptable in the classroom. He knows quite well what behaviors can earn tokens and what behaviors can lose tokens.

Shellie has his head down on his desk and is crying because he has earned no rewards. I feel very sorry for the little fellow as he sits there with his big shoes and empty jar, but I cannot give in to his sorrow, nor to mine. Doing so would only reinforce his crying behavior and his belief that he can manipulate consequences without exerting self-control.

Marcus is watching Shellie intently and comes out of his beloved silence for his friend. He presents what seems to be a reasonable solution.

"Mrs. Evans," he says, "why not allow me to loan some of my tokens to Shellie so that he can get a reward today. When he earns future tokens, he can pay me back."

Shellie raises his head and looks hopeful.

"No," I respond. "That cannot be done."

"But why?" a tearful Shellie asks.

"Because, Shellie, you have to earn your tokens; you can't get rewarded for something someone else has done. If you do not earn tokens, no one will give them to you. As long as you continue to lose tokens you have earned, you will get no rewards. It is entirely up to you. You get what you earn; do not expect something you have not earned."

Does it work? Yes. Next week Shellie earns tokens and is careful not to lose them.

Does it last? No. We have to repeat the process several times over. Even so, Shellie—with his persistence and mine—is accomplishing more and distracting himself and others less.

My job is to teach pro-social and academic skills; it is not to coddle unacceptable behavior. I have found that the combination of positive reinforcement and response cost is beneficial in establishing appropriate behaviors and maintaining control without administering punishment. I have found this Skinnerian strategy to hold true: Behaviors that are rewarded tend to be maintained. Behaviors that are not rewarded (withholding reinforcement) tend to extinguish.[1]

The important task for teachers, parents, and all those in charge of managing others (whether they be adults or children) is to reward only those behaviors we wish to establish and strengthen. We must not reward those behaviors we wish to weaken or eliminate. The problem is that we often—perhaps unknowingly—reward the wrong behaviors. This can be due either to our own inability to be persistent or to our desire to give in to cries and pleas from those who are hurting from lack of reward. Yet, we are hurting them more when we reward them for accomplishments they have not earned.

---

1   Skinner, B.F., *A Matter of Consequences* (New York: Knopf, 1983)

I do admire Marcus's willingness to help his friend. Caring for others, as I told him, is an important part of our existence. (He earns a token for the empathy he displayed.)

"But," as I tried to explain to them all, "no matter how much we care, we cannot give someone else self-confidence, self-respect, or self-control. These are products that come from one's own success in developing competency and achieving goals."

That much-needed feeling of self-worth that these children crave can only come to them through their own efforts and accomplishments. It is true of them as it is true of us all.

"Let us not become weary in doing good, for at the proper time we will reap a harvest if we do not give up."

—Galatians 6:9

STALKY

Run, run, run,
You stalk of bones,
You boy with man-sized woes.

Get away from him
The one inside
Who knows the dreads
And fears you hide.
Who shakes you up
With seriousness
And makes you hyper,
Tight and tense.

Who's your mother?
Who's your father?
Is God in disguise?

Run, run, run,
You've almost won
Your much-sought-after prize.
Gratification,
Instantaneous,
Anxiety-lessening,
Swing on your Tarzan vine.

"It's like swinging on a Tarzan vine," Stalky said, trying to describe the restlessness of being caught between yesterday's discarded childhood and the overwhelming desire for a tomorrow that he feared.

He continued, "I go to my old vine in the backyard and swing like I used to—trying to get that good ole feeling again—but it's gone. I want it back so bad, but it's gone. So I go smoke a little pot and get high. It's kinda like how swinging on that Tarzan vine used to be."

The thought of Stalky swinging on a Tarzan vine with his

fifteen-year-old, long, skinny legs dangling wildly above his size twelve shoes gave me a bittersweet, half-smile.

In the few moments when we were alone and he had been serious, he had told me of his mother who had abandoned him when he was five. His brother was two. "If you own mother don't want you, you feel pretty rotten, you know," he declared. Growing up with this in his mind, he had pretty much managed to abandon others first to avoid further rejection again.

Like Stalky, there was not a child in his group of eight who came from a home where both biological parents were present. These children ranged from ages eleven to fifteen.

THE GROUP

Daniel, fat and shy, was also abandoned by his mother as an infant but lives with loving grandparents who obviously tend to overprotect him. He is fearful and withdrawn.

He—like all children in the group—suffers from childhood neurosis. Childhood neurosis can be considered synonymous with emotional disturbance. It should be differentiated from psychosis, which is a severe mental illness. Neurotic disorders of childhood can take several forms, but the general manifestation is anxiety.

Joey, eleven, is the youngest and smallest of the group. He is extremely pretty. His soft, blond hair is always shiny, and his clothes always clean. He has a habit of compulsively tearing his clean clothes and he seldom says a word. He is a fragile child, looking and acting lost. I do not call on him or force him to make comments in front of others. He had lost his father, whom his mother said he adored, when he was nine. His mother had remarried recently, bringing two more children from that marriage into the home. Since that time, he has developed numerous somatic complaints.

Perhaps it was because he was so small and pretty. Perhaps it was because he never bothered anyone. Perhaps it was just some seldom-shown compassion from the others, but all in the group gave him special accommodations. They would see that he had paper, pencils, and much-needed tenderness. They seemed to recognize the constant reassurance that he needed and gave it to him. I loved that no one ever picked on him or made fun of him.

Teresa, twelve, and her younger sister and two brothers are foster children. She had never seen her mother and had seen her father very few times. She is what clinicians identify as an "acting-out child." She had been labeled as very hard-to-manage and that reputation followed her from year to year, from teacher to teacher. It had become a self-fulfilling prophecy.

Darlene, sixteen, pretty and teasing, told us of how she hated her stepmother and loved her mother. Children so badly need to think that their mothers are good and kind and wonderful even when they have evidence to support the contrary. Darlene's stepmother had pointed out to me at a parent-teacher conference that she was "trying to raise her right." But the harder the stepmother tries, the more Darlene rebels.

Sarah Ann was with her single mom, a cocaine addict, living in squalor. She tried hard with her fourteen-year-old spirit to rise above the ruins of her life. She is an example of a child whose maladjustment comes from her bad environment rather than from internal conflicts.

"As soon as I can get a job, I'm leaving that hell hole," she told us all. School was her only glimpse into normalcy. Education was her only vehicle out of her present state. I reinforced that message every day.

Donald is a country boy—freckled and tanned. Often, he liked to say, "Mrs. Evans, you're crazy."

"School is fun, Donald, I just want you to enjoy it," I replied, as I made a face at him. "I'm not crazy. I just like to hear you laugh every once in a while."

"Yes, you are, Mrs. Evans, you're crazy. I've never seen a teacher like you before."

"Well, tomorrow, I will wear my orthopedic shoes and bring a switch."

"What's orthopedic shoes? Mrs. Evans, you're crazy."

Donald lives with his father and older sister. He does not know why his mother left them; she had been gone for many years. He is burly and muscular from hard farm work.

"I won't be at school next week," he reported to me. "I have to help bale hay, and that ain't no fun. I'd rather be at school."

It was not clear to me why Donald had been referred for placement in a resource class for the emotionally-disturbed even though his referral cited maladaptive behaviors.

His IQ was low average, but he had—according to my observations of him and his verbal descriptions of his life—adapted very well to the conditions under which he lived. His academic achievement was low, and he had been retained at least twice in his school career. Yet, he was a very pleasant and cooperative child.

Jackie was the most emotionally-disturbed of the group and the only one who could be cited as emotionally-disturbed by his appearance. He was thirteen, tall, and lanky. His pants were always too short and his shirts were rumpled as if they needed washing and ironing.

His long, red hair could have been his crowning glory if it were cut and combed rather than being tousled and bedraggled about his lean, pimply face. He was a picture of obvious neglect, if not abuse. His overall disheveled looks coupled with his failure to recognize and comply with commonly-held social standards within the school made him a constant target of ridicule.

It is well-accepted in the field of human development that biological, cultural, and social forces all combine in each of us to make us what we are. It is not as accepted to say that more often than not emotionally-disturbed children come from emotionally-disturbed parents. But in Jackie's case, I believe it to be true.

His mother, whom I had met, was large and loud. She obviously did not adhere to social standards either and seemed to have her own distorted view of reality.

"If Jackie ain't doing right, you just let me know and I will set him straight. You can be sure of that," she loudly proclaimed.

"Jackie is doing fine," I reported to her, not wanting to give her any reason to add more abuse to his already-precarious plight.

The stories Jackie told me concerning her treatment of him

(if correct) were horrendous. He reported that when he was five years old, she held him over a bridge threatening to throw him down into the water.

"What had you done to anger her so?" I asked, knowing, of course, that nothing would justify such harsh punishment on a child.

"I didn't do nothing. She just don't like me and is always trying to scare me, and I am scared of her," he confessed.

"My daddy is scared of her, too; sometimes he stays gone for weeks at a time."

He said on another occasion, when he was a small boy, she had threatened to cut off his penis while holding him down with one hand and holding a knife in the other.

He could have made these stories up himself; I had no proof that they were true. But still, considering his maladjusted-behavior and his neglected appearance, I believed him.

It was after school had dismissed one day that I felt I had reason to act upon my suspicions. He came to my mobile unit and announced that he was not going home. "I am afraid to go home because my mama will kill me."

I stopped what I was doing. "What makes you say that?" I asked.

"Because this morning, she found some red crumbs on my fork and thought I had stuck my fork in the red velvet cake she had made for the church bazaar. I tried to tell her that the crumbs were from red sausages that I had cooked for myself, but she did not believe me and ran me out the door. She said that if I came back, she would kill me."

She made a cake for the church bazaar and threatened to kill her son over it. I wonder what Jesus thinks of that, I thought as I tried to figure out what I could do. It was obviously something I had to take care of now. Once he told me, it became a situation I had to handle. I couldn't leave him at school, and I couldn't take him home with me.

"Wait here," I told him and hurried outside. The auxiliary policeman who was outside directing the car and bus traffic was a friend of mine. I told him I had a child who was afraid to go home and would he please escort him home and check the situation out carefully before leaving him. He was glad to do it.

However, some complications arose. When the policeman called the station to let them know of our plan, he was told that he could not remove a child from school grounds without the parent's permission. (I should have remembered that.)

When I talked by phone to the supervising officer explaining that I thought the child was in danger, he agreed to let the officer bring him to the station and he would call Jackie's mother to come pick him up from there.

"Please do not let him go home with her until you have made it clear that she can be prosecuted for child abuse if she harms him," I begged.

He agreed and called later to assure me that he thought the boy was safe and that he had let him go home with his mother. He also promised to keep a frequent check on the situation.

The next day, Jackie reported to me that his mother did not bother him. "Good," I said while thinking what might happen the next day and the days after that. But, at least, she was now aware that someone was now aware of her. And the authorities would be watching.

"Your children are not your children;
They are the sons and daughters of Life's
Longing for itself.
They come through you but not from you,
And though they are with you, yet they
Belong not to you."

—Kahlil Gibran, *The Prophet*

The Outing

Each outing is an ordeal.

In my resource classroom for these emotionally and socially-maladjusted children, I use a combination of teacher praise, token reinforcement, and response cost as a way of helping them learn that it is they—not I—who must claim responsibility for managing their own behavior.

Each student has a lidded jar on his or her desk. The jar has a slit in the top whereby I can drop in plastic tokens. Students may earn a token for appropriate social and academic behaviors. When explaining the system to them, they work with me on establishing what will be considered appropriate and inappropriate classroom behaviors. Since I am working on their social as well as their academic behaviors, the list must include some of both.

Academic behaviors include being prepared, paying attention, following instructions, working quietly, completing assigned tasks (completion is stressed more than accuracy at the beginning), and asking and answering questions in a reasonable manner.

Social behaviors include getting to class on time, being cooperative, being courteous, showing respect for the teacher and other students, staying in assigned seat during class time, helping others, working without complaints.

Students may lose a token (response cost) for inappropriate behaviors of a negative nature such as making loud noise; using vulgar or rude language; making obscene gestures; breaking class or school rules; displaying aggressive verbal or physical behavior; being out of seat without permission; being late to class; and withdrawal from class activities.

I found this combination of praise, reinforcement, and response cost to be the most effective way of modifying the behaviors of these children.

At the end of the stated period (usually a week), students are allowed to "cash-in" their tokens for special treats or privileges. My sixth period class had been working for a class picnic. When they cashed in their tokens, everyone was eligible.

Our plan was that we would all bring lunch and spend the entire class period on the football field, which was only steps away from the mobile unit. They were all excited and happy that they had earned the right to go.

It was early spring and they needed to feel the sun smiling on their backs and the soft wind caressing their seldom-touched faces with warm friendliness.

The day before, as I was reminding them to bring their lunches, their fears began to surface.

"Everyone will laugh at my lunch," Teresa said with the assurance that comes only from experience.

"We'll look stupid down on the football field having a picnic. What if somebody sees us?" Jackie said, no doubt expressing the feelings of other members of the group.

"My mother won't let me go," Sarah Ann insisted, "because we don't have no groceries in the house."

"Teresa," I offered, "I am going to bring ham and cheese with mayonnaise—my favorite kind of sandwich. If someone laughs at it, I'm just going to eat it anyway because it will still be just as good. I'll bring one for you, Sarah Ann, okay? Or would you rather have another kind?"

"And, Jackie," I continued, "if someone sees us, we will just show them how much fun we're having. It will be fun, you know, getting out of class for one whole hour. Others will probably be envious if they see us."

They all went. Donald said he wanted to play football with the girls, but we all knew he just wanted to roll around in the grass with them. Darlene and Teresa were quite obliging, which required that I keep an eye on them while trying to get Joey down from the top bleacher. He had no lunch. He had probably forgotten and now he was too embarrassed to talk about it, so he separated himself from the rest of us.

Sarah Ann whispered to me, "He has some cheese crackers in his pocket. I saw him get them from the vending machine."

"Hey, Joey," I called. "Have you got some cheese crackers in your pocket? You really do, oh boy! I love cheese crackers. Will you give me one?" He nodded his beautiful little blond head.

"Well, you will have to take a bologna sandwich then. I know you like bologna sandwiches because you told me so. Remember, after school when you go home, you said that you put catsup and mayonnaise and cheese on bologna. Well, how about one without catsup today?"

He smiled a fraction and came down one bleacher.

"Well, here it is," I said as I placed the wrapped sandwich on the next bleacher behind me and the two girls. "Come and get it when you're ready."

Daniel was busy spreading his gourmet mix and getting more attention than he wanted as Joey kept getting closer and closer to his bologna prize.

Sarah Ann kept insisting that I taste her sandwich to prove to the rest of the group that it was not "nasty," which I did. "See, it's good, ain't it, Mrs. Evans?"

"Yes, it's very good, Sarah Ann. I thought you said you had nothing to make sandwiches, so I brought you one."

"Why?" she asked, seeming to forget all about her sad story of yesterday.

"Because I said I would," was my simple reply.

Joey was right behind Daniel now and all were eating and things were going fine.

We had only three rules governing our outing since it was for a short time and such a short distance from our classroom in the mobile unit: stay together, no arguing, and have a good time.

Stalky ran off into the woods after he had smoked under the bleachers. The girls were quick to remind him that his behavior would put him two tokens in the hole. They were right.

But we all left the football field without anyone fighting or crying. It was one of our better outings.

"The important thing is this: to be able at any moment to sacrifice what we are to what we could become."

—Charles Du Bois

THE GREEN CHAIR

The bell sounds and the children come. Frank is the first one in the door. If he gets there first before the others, he will want to sit in the green chair. It is early morning and he is dirty and in yesterday's clothes. "Hi, Frank," I say as he rushes past me to get to the green chair first.

He grunts a greeting and places himself squarely on the sofa. So today, he doesn't feel like an encounter with Randy over the green chair.

"Are you gonna let Randy sit in the green chair today?" He asked me.

"It's Randy's day, Frank. You can check the chart," I answered matter-of-factly.

"Well, you said if we missed our day, we lost our turn, and Randy missed his turn yesterday," he hissed accusingly. For me to go against my word would reinforce his long-held belief that adults are not to be trusted.

"Yes, that's true, Frank. I'm glad you remember so well. But you must also remember that the rule states if you miss your day due to school time, you get your turn. We didn't meet this class yesterday because of the assembly schedule. That wasn't Randy's fault. We have to honor the agreement."

He knew it as well as I did. But he needed the reassurance that nobody was getting special treatment, so I gave it to him.

Stanley comes in halfway through my explanation to Frank and says, "Mrs. Evans, I told you to throw the green chair out and solve the problem."

"Throwing the green chair out doesn't solve the problem, Stanley," I responded. "Throw it out; run away from it; blame it on somebody else—that is all so much easier than dealing with it. We must deal with situations and try to resolve them as they arise."

The green chair, as ridiculous as it is to others, is very important to these kids. They have made it a place of prestige. It has become the desired position in the room sought after by all except Stanley, Elaine, and Devon.

Randy had demanded the chair every day. No matter who got there first, he would try to bully, buy, or threaten his way into the chair. He did not like to be close to the others.

Consequently, it became a seat of power; those who sat in it were able to defy Randy. Randy was the handsome one; the well-dressed one; the one from an upscale family.

Randy, who at seventeen drove his own car to school, presented himself to be well-versed in women, cars, and good times. He considered himself to be far better than the rest of them and they knew it. His arrogance and disdain made the others feel even more unattractive and less confident than they already felt. But, Randy has his own problems: He is a defiant, under-achieving narcissist who is rejected by his peers and most of his teachers.

When Phillip, big and husky, and tired of being pushed around by this "pretty-boy," as he called him, offered to fight Randy for the chair, I decided it was time for me to step in.

So after a complete full-period session of discussion, we all agreed on a seating chart and some rules of governance. (*I could have done it in half the time, but it is important to let the students have input into rules by which they must abide. By doing so, they will feel some ownership and, of course, I will always remind them that they agreed to the rules.*)

Each person who wanted to add his name to the list would take turns sitting in the green chair. If they were absent from class on their day, that would forfeit their right until the next time around. But, if they missed their day due to a school change or due to my absence (which had never happened) they could have their turn the following day. It sounds very simple. But it was not simple to them. Over the weekend they would forget who sat in it last. Some would insist that they had not had their turn. That's why I kept an accurate chart.

"Throw it out," was Stanley's suggestion. "You sit in it, Mrs. Evans," was Elaine's. But they all agreed to the system. If they all followed the simple rules and respected one another's rights, perhaps they would learn that compromise and rules do make a difference in conflicting matters. Some wanted to give away their day when they didn't feel like being seen for one reason or another. If this happened, who would get to sit in the chair? "No one would sit in the chair; it would remain empty," I had declared. Phillip was called to the office during his day, so who sits in it? "No one will sit in the chair; it will remain empty," I declared again.

They would argue among themselves. But they all knew that I would not cheat them. So whenever a question arose, they trusted me to settle it. They did not trust me automatically. I worked long and hard to gain that trust.

Trust, being the most important ingredient in any relationship, is absolutely essential in working with these children. If they feel that they can't trust me, I may as well stay home. But when the trust is there, they will listen and believe. When they see trust in action, they may learn to respect its powerful force in the relationships they will build as they grow outward from the mobile unit and the green chair.

Randy strolled in and announced: "I sit in the green chair today because we didn't have this class yesterday."

"That is absolutely right," I said. "We all agree. No one can argue with that because that's the way our system works. See how much easier life is when we all follow a few simple rules."

Some of the children were actually disappointed because they had nothing to sulk about. But, class had only begun.

Devon came in late and lay down near the wall and covered his face. "Are you going to join us today, Devon?" I asked without sarcasm.

"Not today, Mrs. Evans. I feel rough."

"Okay," I said.

"He'll lose two tokens for withdrawl, won't he, Mrs. Evans?" chimed in Elaine.

"Yes, it's his choice and his points," I said. "The subject is closed."

Many of these teenagers were sent to me because they were "behavior problems" in the regular classrooms. They had to be managed. Or, as I choose to tell them, "You manage yourself in here. You're honest with me. I'm honest with you. We play no games. We tell it like it is. You are accountable for your own behavior and will reap the consequences of that behavior. I am here to help you help yourself. But it is you who make the choices of what you will do, how you will behave, what you will strive for."

"I am my choices."

—Jean-Paul Sartre

I AM MATTHEW

"Come in," I said to the knock at the door as I unscrewed the top of my coffee thermos.

"Hi, did you say come in?" he asked.

"Yes," I replied. "You must be Phillip."

"No," he said as he looked very confident and straight at me. "I am Matthew."

"Oh, I'm sorry," I smiled. "Phillip is a new referral that I am expecting this week. I have no referral on you, Matthew."

His dark eyes scanned quickly over the room and rested questioningly on the student's desk pushed up in front of mine. I motioned for him to sit down.

"Thank you," he said smiling. His teeth were glistening white and even. His athletic-looking frame was surely out of place as he tried to fit it into the tired, old desk, which must have been built for a fourth grader. But his face still held a sparkle of confidence. He was an immaculately well-dressed, nice-looking boy. I guessed him to be about seventeen.

"So you mean that you must have a referral before you can work with students? I thought you had walk-in time available to anyone."

"Well, I have had walk-in time in years past. I would save a period a day for that purpose. My first year out here in this mobile unit I held workshops about three times a week open to the entire school population, and students could come during study hall. But now, I have all six periods filled with regular students who have been referred and must come each day. State Department of Education requirements about contact time and such things have eliminated walk-in time."

"Oh, I see," he said. "Cathy told me that you used to spend an hour a week with her during her senior year, and that it meant a lot."

"Yes, that was two years ago. Cathy is now a sophomore in college—working on tomorrow."

I had thirty minutes for lunch each day. I glance at my watch. Now I had twenty.

"Well, Matthew, I'll tell you what. I've got twenty minutes left. Let's go over and sit there," I said as I nodded toward the worn brown sofa and dark green upholstered chair, "If you can stand my munching on this apple, we can get acquainted."

He smiled in agreement as he happily removed himself from the small desk. Sure, I could have sent him away. It probably would have been the sensible thing to do. I had been going four straight periods with no breaks and I had already decided that I was not the Messiah. But this young man looked as if he might be in better shape than I was and probably just wanted to kill some time.

"Mrs. Evans, I feel kinda bad taking your lunch time," he said. I felt this was a sincere statement—rather than a fabricated whine. (I had learned to distinguish the difference.)

"It's okay. Whether you were here or not, I would still have just this apple."

"Have you had lunch?" I asked.

"Yes, thank you. I'm fine."

Usually, when students come in on their own, there is a little embarrassment in presenting themselves for help. The first thing I do is try to put them at ease. But he immediately took the role of initiating conversation. "You have a nice place here," he said. "Do you like it?"

I gave the wiggly hand in the air and wrinkled my nose as a reply. He laughed.

I added, "I do feel that it is a worthwhile place, although sometimes it does get difficult out here. I have made a lot of real good relationships like with Cathy whom you mentioned earlier. We shared a lot of good thoughts."

"Yes, I know," he said with a serious tone to his voice. "Perhaps, I want a little of that realness. Maybe that's why I'm here."

"Maybe so," I said. "We can explore ideas and toss around philosophies. Or, perhaps, we will talk of cabbages and kings."

"Yes," he said smiling again, "or mice and men. Or maybe I can just come out here to water my leaves when I am thirsty for truth."

"Is there a poet beneath the sun-tanned skin?" I asked.

He gave me back the wiggly hand in the air and we both laughed. It was happening already: It is that good comfortable, universal feeling that knows no age, no race, no gender. It is a natural person-to-person contact that makes real communication possible.

The bell rang.

"Oh, darn," he said. "I just got here."

"Well, there's always tomorrow. Bring your own apple and we will have thirty minutes."

"All right," he said. "And thanks, Mrs. Evans."

"My pleasure," I said—and meant it.

He came in the next day with his apple. "You know, some people call me Matt."

"You are Matthew," I replied. "You said so yourself with such dignity and pride. Matt is okay. I prefer Matthew."

"Me, too," he nodded. "I am Matthew—not Matt. I really don't like shortened names or any unnecessary short-cuts."

"Why would anyone take an unnecessary short-cut, Matthew?" I asked, genuinely curious about such a remark.

"It's due to laziness and easy ways out. Do you cheat, Mrs. Evans?"

"No, I don't cheat, Matthew. But, I have cheated. The reason I don't cheat now—as trite as it may sound—is now I know that when you cheat at something, you are only cheating yourself."

"Why didn't you tell me that you had never cheated. I would have believed you."

"Well, to lie about it would be cheating now. Failure to accept the truth about yourself is cheating yourself. One must face the truth. The truth is reality and we must deal with truth. Now is a good time to say a little about that. I never pry; I never expect you or anyone else to tell me anything. Coming out here puts you under no obligation to tell me anything you do not want to share.

"But, what you do say must always be the truth. The truth is all we have. And, of course, I will always keep what you share confidential, unless, of course, you are engaged in some illegal activity or you tell me that you or are planning to harm yourself or someone else."

"Oh, no argument from me on that. And by the way, I have never cheated. Just keep that in mind, okay?"

"Sure," I nodded. And I was to keep that in mind throughout the days ahead.

"There were so many reasons why I wanted to come and talk to you," he continued. "But what finally brought me out here yesterday was cheating: cheating in the classroom. It makes me sick to my stomach. Mrs. Evans, you would be surprised if you knew how many so-called good students—honor students—are cheating their way through every class they have."

I had heard that story before. I remember Julie who cried about it. She sobbed and sobbed because it was so unfair. She went to the Board of Education with that and much more—three years ago.

"What can I do about it, Mrs. Evans?"

"As I see it, here are your alternatives: You can report the students to the classroom teachers; you can approach the students themselves; or, you can write it up as their loss and not yours. Do you have any other suggestions, Matthew? Wearing yourself out, getting sick over the situation is hurting you. They should be suffering for their dishonor, not you. But then, that doesn't solve the problem I know. Let's brainstorm ideas."

He sat quietly, offering nothing.

After a minute or so, I gave him my suggestion: "Why don't you write an editorial in the school newspaper about cheating?"

"That last idea suits me better. I like to write anyway—especially my opinion," he laughed. "As a matter of fact, I wrote something last night. I wanted to share it with you."

"Wonderful! Let's hear it."

He reached in his back pocket and pulled out a neatly-folded piece of notebook paper. He began: *What is it that I aspire to? What would give me satisfaction of a lasting endurance? Why must I step to a pace that is heard so seldom by so few? Why do I love the solitude of my songs more than I care for the sound of the chorus? Who gave me this measure so far away? Will I ever know the essence of me? Where do I go from now?*

By the time he had reached the last question, his voice had taken on a pensive, full sound. He finished and sat there looking down at his hands.

It was a tense moment for us both. This beautiful, sad boy— whose intelligence may well have exceeded my own—was going to cry. The bell was going to ring, and my fifth period was coming in.

Trying to relieve the tension, I said in a low voice, "Matthew, you don't expect me to answer all these questions today do you?"

He smiled and looked slightly relieved, but said, "I expect somebody to answer them."

The old reliable bell rang.

"I guess I got to go, right?"

"Yes, you have to go. We are slaves of the bell around here. But, we will work to find these answers. We will search. Write some more."

"I will. Bye now." He folded his treasured questions together carefully, neatly, as if his troubled thoughts could rest if he locked them inside the safety of the folded paper.

"Here," he said as he handed me the little bundle of paper and ink and anguish. "You keep everything. You keep it all 'til next time."

"Write that editorial," I called to him as he went out the door.

**"Our chief want is someone who will inspire
us to be what we know we could be."**

—Ralph Waldo Emerson

FIFTH PERIOD

My fifth period came in: Janet with her bushy, long hair limping past my desk to get my attention. I chose not to ask her about the elastic wrap around her ankle. Tomorrow it would be another malady she had invented. So desperately she wants attention.

Rachel was close behind her. Rachel is always trying to hide behind someone. She does not talk. She does not want anyone to talk to her. She is an elective mute.

Once a child is referred for psychological testing and educational evaluation, and parental permission is obtained, the interdisciplinary team begins its due process work. School nurses will check the child for possible auditory, visual, or speech impairments. After which, a school social worker will go into the home to interview the parents or caregivers. In addition, they must get written permission from the parent or surrogate to secure a copy of the child's medical records. (Some children have no medical records.)

In reviewing Rachel's social and medical history, I find no physiological cause for her lack of speech. Also, there is nothing recorded to indicate psychological trauma. Her mother reports that around the age of five years, "she just stopped talking."

But, Rachel has not stopped talking entirely. She talks to Maggie. She talks only to Maggie; therefore, Maggie speaks for her. Their relationship is fascinating to me. Rachel is a frail, little Caucasian girl of nine years. Her pale, blond hair is very thin and straight. Her appearance reeks of undernourishment or possible poverty. Yet, I have no written (or oral) information in school records to verify this.

Maggie, also nine, is a healthy, vibrant African-American child who has never been referred to me. They are in all classes together except for mine. It seems that everyone accepts the fact that if you want to know what Rachel thinks or wants, you have to ask Maggie. Going through the lunch line Maggie will tell the lunchroom ladies what food items to put on Rachel's tray. I have watched them sitting together at lunch. They are chattering away. But as soon as someone approaches, Rachel will become mute and keep her eyes fixed on Maggie.

Maggie brings Rachel to the mobile unit each day. Before she departs for her own class, she will give me any pertinent information I should know about Rachel. Information such as: "Rachel is not feeling well today. She has an upset stomach, so she may have to leave class for the bathroom." Or, "Rachel has a math test today; she needs for you to go over fractions and percentages with her."

I appreciate this information from Maggie, but I do not allow her to come in and sit with Rachel. One of my stated goals on Rachel's Individualized Education Plan is to increase her self-reliance and oral communication. (It appears to me that Maggie enjoys "taking care" of Rachel and actually reinforces Rachel's need for her.) Yet, this has to be handled very carefully; Rachel is very fragile and I must not move too fast.

Carlton, who has been called "Humpty Dumpty" for years by some of his classmates, sits himself comfortably on the sofa. He will close his eyes and withdraw if I, or a classmate, do not want to hear about his imagined car today. If you are called "Humpty-Dumpty" because your large head sits atop your shoulders—seemingly without a neck for support—and you know something about every car on the road—that is the most important thing in your life.

Right before the tardy bell stopped ringing, Terry blows in with her funny face and giggle. Giggling is her constant companion. She emits that high-pitched giggle for no apparent reason, at the most inappropriate times. Perhaps, it fills the void she feels within herself.

Clifford comes in slowly, caring not that he is tardy. Clifford appears to care for little; he seems to exist to torture others. Children who torture others have been tortured themselves.

Yes, all are much different from Matthew, who looks as if he should be featured in *All-American Youth* magazine. But humanity passes our way in all kind of shapes and forms and needs. Somehow, I was to take each of these little remnants and by some excellent training or magic potion produce lessons that would meet all their needs. And they each deserve the best I can offer. My desire to help these misshaped children will no doubt always outweigh my ability to do so.

Maybe someday I would believe the words I have heard from others more experienced than I. Words meant to encourage: "Do all you can and forget it."

"They developed these problems for many years now and you can't eliminate them in one school year. You expect too much of these children."

"You have to be satisfied with a little progress."

"You have to present over and over the same idea. You think they have learned it, but they haven't."

I know that words, alone, do not teach. Experience teaches. How limited are their experiences in the mobile unit one hour each day.

**"Do nothing out of selfish ambition or vain conceit.
Rather, in humility value others above yourselves,
not looking to your own interests but . . .
. . . to the interests of the others."**

—Philippians 2:3-4 (NIV)

MATTHEW RETURNS

When I got to school the next morning, I found this note slipped under my locked door. It read: *"Public school education is a sore which has become diseased; it will eventually die."*

Of course, I knew its author. Since I had only thirty minutes to spend with Matthew one day a week, he had chosen to communicate his thoughts through written notes. He would leave a note slipped under my door on Monday. (We did not have e-mail at that time.) Then, by Thursday, we would talk about those thoughts he had written. He could get my reaction; I could get his. He never wrote happy little notes. Usually he wrote long, searching messages that lingered and haunted me through the day (and sometimes nights in between). He never wrote the editorial on cheating. When I questioned him about it, he replied, "I concluded that it is not my problem."

On Monday morning, I found Matthew's second writing slipped under my door. It read: *"I love the woods; they are so vast and enduring. The trees have long since seen many such as I come and go. Yet, they remain durable and majestic.*

I envy Thoreau who stayed so much longer than I and wrote with such brilliance. The world is a long way off from me. I can faintly hear the large trucks on the highway.

I care so little for so much that I do. I spend so much time doing so many things that I am tired of doing. The only thing I require is time alone. Within the solitary confinement of my depths I go to explore and find and seek again. I ask for little: no costly pursuit—no person to praise me. I seek only to know from within my soul the solitary thoughts that spring.

In the woods, I am absolutely alone. Nothing is after me to get done. No one is calling my name. The sun is there only for me. The breeze is nippy and gently stings my face as it whispers by me. The odd-shaped trees are beautiful—more beautiful than any living thing.

Bright green ferns spring up here and there. I just heard a 'caw-caw,' as a crow soared overhead.

It matters little here if one is successful or not. What do the trees care? Riches, position, and fame are like the dead leaves of winter which the wind tosses along the ground. The earth cares little for your daily doses of work and worry. She claims your body to feed her growth and life goes onward. You are not so important to the woods. She shares with you as she shares with the squirrels and rabbits. You are no more than they.

I come to the woods just to be. There is no adrenalin running through my body. I am calm and beautifully free. I do not want to go back to the outer world. The sun is warm and the leaves are still. Brown and tired and still. I am a leaf waiting for spring. Spring in the woods is breathtaking. Spring in my heart, will it come?"

Matthew came in Thursday promptly at 12:10. "How did you like the woods?" he asked. There was no hello, no gradual warming up. Just "how did you like the woods?"

"I liked the woods very much," I replied. "I go there quite often myself. As a matter of fact, I feel much the same way you do about the peacefulness and majesty of the woods. Your writing is beautiful. I think you are very talented. You should continue to write—always write. You mentioned Thoreau. Who is another writer who has inspired you?"

"I particularly like Kahlil Gibran," he said.

"Oh, yes, the Lebanese poet. You no doubt have read Gibran's *The Prophet*."

He nodded.

"Well, from your readings you see there are those who step in time to your beat, Matthew. You're not alone. But I can't ignore the message your words conveyed to me. The tendency to withdraw is not that unusual. We all need to withdraw from over-stimulation.

"We need to be alone to explore the hollows of our hearts and the depths of our soul. But we withdraw in order to emerge revived. I understand your need for withdrawal; it is even healthy and necessary for creative minds. But you don't want to withdraw into yourself too much. It can become unhealthy. Just thought I would mention that. Do you understand?"

"Yes," he said. "I understand that. It's just that I enjoy solitude more than I enjoy company. Most kids my age are interested in stupid stuff. Like who's got the weed or the booze, or who hooked up with who over the weekend. Sometimes, I wish I could be like that. But more often than not, I pity them, and I am glad to realize that there is more to life than making out and getting high."

"Teenage years, Matthew, are a time for exploration, for seeking, for establishing one's identity. Persons just handle their role confusion in different ways. Some are more introverted—requiring aloneness; others more extroverted—requiring company. There are other teenagers like you, Matthew. We are a small school here. There is not a lot of variety. But in a large school, like college, you will meet others like you. But here, you could exert your influence and become a much-needed leader. I'm sure that respect and—"

He interrupted me, "I have tried a lot of things here. Sports. I'm good at basketball. I play tennis—not too well yet. I instruct swimming and serve as a lifeguard at the community pool. I signed up for classes here to find them just boring. I joined the marching band, which was a big mistake. I've tried the drama club . . . no good. I really don't think it's all me. I honestly think the whole world is going to 'hell in a hand basket.' I guess I am too wholesome, you know, like the American flag and apple pie." He offered an awkward laugh at that.

But there was no hint of laughter in his next written communication left under my door:

Depression is an ugly woman with a dark, heavy shawl which she throws around me. It engulfs me; I am drawn into the deepness. In the entanglement of this heavy shawl, I go back into all the old pits which I have frequented before.

I know it will lift and I wait for the pain in my head to lessen. I wait for the ache in my soul to subside. I wonder what damage she had done this time to my psyche—what scars this time to heal. What hurt this time?

How many sunny days will it take to dry the tears? How many warm nights to melt the cold? How many walks in the woods to remind me that someday it won't matter?

Depression is an ugly woman who comes again and again to rob me of my youth, my vitality, my hope, my faith. I understand this lonely, ugly woman. She is just looking for comfort, for love, for company. She gnaws at me as she generates self-pity. Seductively, she tells me to join her. She reminds me that she is my old friend, the only one who understands me. Bit by bit, she gnashes her carnivorous teeth into my flesh and laughs as I follow her into the darkness.

I cannot fight off this old ugly demon who reminds me over and over again that there is no truth but hers. "Poor little boy," she says to me. "Don't you know that the fools who are happy are ignorant? Many have trod your path seeking truth only to be overtaken by the masses. Only a fool wants to continue to push and shove without reward."

Matthew came in at his usual time on Thursday; he was not wearing a smile. He walked in quietly and went to the green chair.

"Matthew," I began, "I like the way you chose to personify depression. I'm not trying to critique your writing. I am just trying to be where you are. You have made depression into something tangible. Do you see that by being tangible, depression becomes something you can attack—a demon you can fight off?"

"Yes," he answered. "I think so."

He continued: "As depression leaves me slowly, I am weakened and empty. The void must be filled. If it does not fill, next time she will weaken me even more. Like an unattended wound in my flesh, depression infects my entire body making it diseased. And she will be back. She comes less frequently now, but she will be back."

"You are feeling sorry for yourself, Matthew." I paused to watch his facial expression. "Don't be alarmed. I feel sorry for myself at times, too. Perhaps, all do at one time or another. Yet, you and I both know that self-pity is the glory of depression. It keeps us down. Tell me what makes you feel sorry for yourself, Matthew."

"The whole damn world depressed me because it is evil. I don't like it and I don't fit in."

"The whole world is not evil, Matthew. Think of all the schools, the churches, the organizations and people who are reaching out to help others. Much of humanity glows with such goodness. I'm sure you can think of those you know who are good and kind. Tell me of one."

He shook his head. "No."

I continued, "Look at the prophet, Gibran, who sings to you familiar songs. Look inside yourself. Have patience with the world. Sing your songs and write your poems. Do not let life beat you down. It is not what happens to us, but how we perceive what happens to us that determines its effect. Think of this: If we let times be ordinary, the times will not fill us. If we see only that which is visible, we become spiritually blind. If we feel only that which is tangible, we are shallow. If we believe only that which is evident, we are faithless. If we become unproductive and uncreative, we are a tomb, a shell of death."

He showed no signs of agreement. However, despite his despairing utterances, I don't believe Matthew to be clinically depressed. I believe his bouts of depression can be lessened and finally dissolved with a change in cognition and behavior.

Irrational thinking can bring about depression. Or, depression can bring about irrational thinking.

Whichever the case may be, I know that changing our faulty thinking into more logical and reasonable beliefs helps to abolish self-defeating thoughts. If we can revise our irrational beliefs, we can gain more control of our life.

"Quick," I said hastily, "name five things that you believe to be beautiful and good."

He started slowly, "Apples," he said.

Then he added with a little more enthusiasm, "Girls with nice bodies and sweet smiles." He continued slowly showing some degree of interest: "Children playing happily; teachers who care; clean, babbling water flowing over smooth rocks in a stream."

He paused and then added playfully, "One more thing—maybe even this old green chair. This old green chair gives me a comfortable place to be."

"Well, yes. Someone else may see it as very ugly and useless, but that someone does not know what it means to you. If you perceive it to be beautiful, then beautiful it is to you."

**"The mind is its own place, and in itself
can make a heav'n of hell, a hell of heav'n."**

—John Milton

It should be noted that if one suffers from an organic mental disorder, or from a chemical imbalance of neurotransmitters in the brain, or psychoactive substance addiction, such conditions consist of more than cognitive aspects. In which case, medication is most often required.

Psychiatrists, who are medical doctors, are authorized to prescribe drugs such as tranquilizers and antidepressants. Both psychiatrists and psychologists deal with psychological and emotional disorders. But those psychologists, who are not medical doctors, cannot prescribe drugs.

Matthew reports that he had formerly made one visit to a psychiatrist. He said the doctor conversed with him very little before quickly writing out a prescription for drugs. He wanted someone to listen to his symptoms and try to treat the issues he described. He did not, as he said, "want to be just another person who was overmedicated." He reportedly dropped the written prescription in the trash can on his way out the door and never went back.

Since he says there is no one in his family with a history of depression, this rules out the likelihood that he has a biological or genetic predisposition to depression. Therefore, he appears to be a person whose problems are transitory and can be eliminated—or at least decreased—by changing his way of thinking and his belief systems. Rational-emotive therapists hold that abnormal behavior often emerges from irrational beliefs.[1]

I believe this is true of Matthew. By changing his cognitions with more favorable thoughts and more realistic beliefs, his psychological well-being can improve.

"All that a man achieves and all that he fails to achieve is the direct result of his own thoughts."

—James Allen

---

1   Ellis, A., *Humanistic Psychotherapy: The Rational-Emotive Approach,* (New York: McGraw-Hill, 1973)

Matthew was sitting in the green chair when my fifth period arrived. I had noticed, on other occasions, that he seemed to be especially drawn to Rachel. Today, prior to leaving, he walked over to her desk to give her the apple that he had not eaten. He said nothing, just placed the apple on her desk. She did not move until he was out the door. Then she picked up the apple and carefully placed it in her bookbag.

Each Thursday thereafter, Matthew would always give something to Rachel before he left. Once, it was a pencil and pocket calendar; another time, it was a peppermint stick. It was always something small that she could easily carry in her bookbag. He never said anything to her; he just placed his little gifts on her desk.

Matthew had asked me if it was all right for him to do that, and I told him "yes." I had noticed that Rachel was beginning to look at him in eager anticipation of his gifts. Once, she even smiled at him and he smiled back.

I am so grateful when the children begin to respond to one another. They often can reach where I cannot go. Peer acceptance—which I cannot give them—is very important to a child. Some developmental psychologists have postulated that beginning in middle school, peer acceptance becomes even more important to a child than parental acceptance. Of course, there are always some exceptions.

**"Blessed are they who have the gift of making friends,
for it is one of God's best gifts."**
—Thomas Hughes

VALENTINE'S DAY

Valentine's Day is particularly hard for the emotionally-disturbed child in a school setting. The school is often aglow with balloons, flowers, stuffed animals, and pretty boxes of candy. They see their classmates receiving red and pink envelopes symbolizing the love and affection they so badly want. But they, more often than not, do not receive such celebratory packages. This only reinforces their low self-esteem; they see it as proof of their unworthiness. I always bring valentines for all of them, so at least they will have one.

And, of course, I had one for Matthew. But, he did not need mine. Even though he decries that he does not fit in, his classmates and teachers love him. He comes in with dozens of valentines, and he has not even met all his classes for the day. He is not particularly excited about all the valentines he has received. What he is excited about is the one he plans to give Rachel.

He shows it to me. It is perfect. He has chosen carefully. He does not—as he confesses to me—want her to think that he is her "boyfriend." Those who are needy and dependent can often become overly-attached to anyone who is considerate and nice to them. He is instinctively aware of this; I do not have to explain it to him. The valentine has a pretty vase of pink and yellow flowers on the front. Inside is simply, "Happy Valentine's Day." He signed it, "Your Friend, Matthew.'

I am so touched by his concern for this little muted waif-of-a-child, but I am not surprised. Matthew is an intellectually-gifted young man who is sensitive. The gifted are often sensitive. They view life from an internal perception that is uncommon. They pick up easily on sights and sounds around them that others may miss. This keen perception allows them to see sorrow as well as beauty.

Oftentimes, too, they can be depressed—as is Matthew. This is not to say that all depressed people are gifted, nor is it to imply that all gifted are depressed.

Yet, the truly gifted are acutely aware that they are different from the masses—as does Matthew. I have found that the giving of oneself to meaningful purpose is one of the best antidotes for depression and serves the gifted well.

I am convinced that Matthew will find his purpose, and he will pursue it with passion. How fortunate am I to be the one he selected to help him find that purpose.

Matthew waited until the fifth period students came in and were seated. He walked over to Rachel as he usually does. Rather than laying today's valentine gift card on her desk as usual, he held it out before her. She reached for it. She actually reached for it. He smiled and turned to leave.

We all heard it. It was soft and low, but it was clearly audible. Rachel said, "Thank you."

"The meeting of two personalities is like the contact of two chemical substances; if there is any reaction, both are transformed."

—Carl Jung

CREATING A MONSTER

Sarah Jean was not obese; she was just big. She could, I suppose, be classified—as my Aunt Ola had described herself—"big-boned."

She had, as expected, the demeanor of one who is very dissatisfied with her appearance. As females become older they are able to make compensation for what they deem an unattractive physical appearance. We have all known those who were not physically attractive but whose intellect, vivaciousness, or overall disposition gave them charisma of lasting significance. But when you are a middle-school girl who longs to be one of the cute little cheerleaders, or one of the ones who has a boyfriend, it is a long, hard journey to adulthood.

Her mother brought her to me after a parent-teacher conference with her science teacher. "Mrs. Conner told me to bring Sarah Jean to you," her mother said as an introduction. I cannot determine if teachers send their unusual students to me because of the confidence they place in my being able to deal with "exceptionalities" or if it is because they simply do not want to deal with these students' peculiar behaviors themselves. It matters little, I suppose, because once they come through the door, they are mine. And I accept them.

I am often amazed how some mothers—in their child's presence—will talk about that child in such negative terms as they try to describe the presenting problems. Many times, I fathom, it is a defensive need to cling to their own image of "the good mother" in spite of having raised this problem child. And, of course, they always want help for the child whom they deem is the problem.

Sarah Jean towered over her slim, well-groomed mother by several inches. There was a striking contrast between her appearance and that of her mother's. The difference seemed to add to her unusually large size and unkempt appearance.

"I can't do anything with her," she began. "She's failing all her classes and sometimes she just refuses to go to school at all. When she does go, she comes home from school, goes into her room, and locks the door. She stays there all afternoon and she won't let me in. She won't talk to me or her dad and she never goes anywhere with friends. I don't think she has any friends."

"Does she have siblings?" I asked.

"No," her mother replied. "It's just her."

I was watching Sarah Jean as her mother continued to describe her in these not-so-glowing terms. During most of her mother's narrative, she just looked at the floor. There were two times that she looked up and rolled her eyes. She did look at me once and shake her head "No" as her mother reported that she thought she was taking some kind of drugs and that is why she would not let her in.

"When did this behavior you are describing begin?" I asked her mother.

"We used to have such fun together when she was a little girl," she replied ignoring my question.

"How old are you, Sarah Jean?" I asked.

"She just turned fourteen," her mother quickly responded. "We were going to give her a party, but she did not want one."

"You recognize," I said to her mother whose name I did not yet know, "that she has entered adolescence and is undergoing lots of changes. Some of these changes may be hard for her."

"Well, it's hard for me, too," she declared with annoyance.

I wanted to talk with Sarah Jean and did not need to allow her mother to continue ranting. "Sarah Jean," I said, "I will see you tomorrow at 12:00 noon. Is that your lunch time? I don't want to intrude on your lunch time."

"I don't eat lunch," she said. "I can come then."

"That's another thing," her mother added. "She is trying to lose weight and hardly eats enough to keep herself alive."

"Well, stay alive until tomorrow, Sarah Jean," I said. She smiled, but her mother did not seem to catch my humorous attempt to lessen the tension.

"I certainly hope you can help her. I've done all I know to do and am at my wit's end," her mother said as she prepared to leave.

"I certainly hope so, too. Goodbye for now."

From my session with Sarah Jean the following day, she described her mother as overbearing and critical.

"She is always on me about my size. She is the one who has been after me for several years now to lose weight. But I just can't lose any. My two girl cousins are small and slim like their mother and mine, and she is always comparing me to them."

"What about school?" I asked.

"I hate school. I wish I didn't have to come at all." She began crying. "Most of the boys make fun of me, and I really don't have a good friend in this whole school."

"How do the boys make fun of you?" I asked. "Tell me what they say."

"They call me 'booger-woman' and say things like 'let's go out tonight, booger-woman,' and laugh."

"What do you do when they say such things?" I asked.

"I don't say anything. I just walk away."

"You make no comment at all?"

"No. Once, when we were walking into English class, John Strickland said, 'Get out of my way, booger-woman,' and Mrs. Jules, our teacher, laughed herself."

"Would you describe these boys as aggressive?"

"Yes."

"Would you describe yourself as passive since you just walk away?"

"Yes."

"Describe to me how it feels to be passive when someone is acting aggressive toward you."

"It feels awful."

"Would you like to learn a more effective way of dealing with those who are aggressive toward you?"

"Yes."

Bullying has always been abound in schools. We pay attention to it now because too many tragic incidents of bullying have been called to our national attention—especially since social media came upon us. We have learned that those who are bullied sometimes end the torture by taking their own lives. In addition, those who are bullied can also retaliate in such a way as to rein unrestrained terror down on the innocent.

Just as Sarah Jean has said, "it feels awful to be bullied." She, however, without realizing it allows herself to be easy prey.

Submissive, passive persons are easy targets. If we respond aggressively, we become a bully ourselves. Assertiveness is our best defense against others' aggressive behavior.

If one can learn assertiveness, one will fare much better. Unlike aggressiveness, which seeks to hurt others, assertiveness shows respect for others. At the same time, it affords oneself the same respect as shown to others. Passiveness, on the other hand, reduces our self-esteem by allowing others to bully us, walk over us, or take advantage of us. Self-respect is not brought about by submission to others' demands. Nor can we acquire self-worth by "feeling awful." Sarah Jean's feeling of self-worth is very low for a variety of reasons.

Some factors no doubt include how she assesses her physical appearance. Her mother's behavior toward her and her lack of friends in the school environment all tend to add to her devaluation of herself. Self-esteem plays an important role in our mental health. How we view ourselves spills over into much that we do—or don't do.

I chose to begin by illustrating assertiveness. Sarah Jean and I go through many sessions of assertiveness training. We even have acting-out skits to portray the difference in assertiveness, aggressiveness, and passiveness. In our role-playing, sometimes I am the aggressor; other times, it is she who becomes the aggressor. We act out passive, aggressive, and assertive ways to respond to an aggressor.

I realize that the security of the mobile unit is unlike the atmosphere she encounters in other school settings. When several of your peers are surrounding you with insults, it is much more difficult to apply skills you have learned in a safe environment. Yet, we must practice in order for this transfer to be remotely possible.

Several weeks had passed when the assistant principal in

charge of discipline called me in. He laughingly said to me, "Mrs. Evans, you have created a monster."

"What do you mean?" I asked.

"That shy, never-causing-any-trouble girl named Sarah Jean just punched John Strickland, who was calling her booger-woman, to the floor and told all the others with him to go to hell."

I felt rather defeated. Glad was I that the shy, submissive girl was no longer "feeling awful." But clearly, Sarah Jean had not learned the difference between aggressiveness and assertiveness. Or, she had chosen to retaliate with aggression of her own. And I thought we had done so well.

It was time now to work on other aspects of her feelings of poor self-worth. Yet, I must admit as I walked back to the mobile unit, I had a feeling of satisfaction by thinking that those boys are less likely to bother her again. But, at the same time, I knew that when aggression is reinforced by terminating an undesirable behavior in others, it will increase the likelihood that aggression will be used in other situations.

Perhaps I had created a monster. And I thought we had done so well.

"And faintly trust the larger hope."

—Alfred Lord Tennyson

"Just Once"

As I approached the mobile unit I saw there were no obscene pictures on my steps this morning glaring at me in their rawness.

That, in itself, was an improvement over yesterday. Located at the rear of the main school building, my unit was easily accessible to early school arrivals who fought their boredom through stolen cigarettes and adolescent fantasy.

But, I reminded myself—as I so often must—this is not the whole picture. I had found other things on my steps. Once there had been two live bunnies in a cardboard box with a note attached: "Mrs. Evans, please keep these for me 'til after school. Love, Joey."

And it was a warm day in September when the King-Kong glass sat there fiercely holding a bouquet of soft, wild flowers gleaming in its anonymity.

But mostly, I found children waiting there—children waiting for an unlocked door.

The mobile unit is a safe sanctuary. They find acceptance here. In addition, I want it to be a place where they find hope. I want them to be able to go forth without fear.

As the six students in my first period class of the day began entering, David came in singing loudly. It wasn't hip-hop—or rowdy rap—as one might expect. It was that beautiful soul ballad, "Just Once," recorded by James Ingram. I looked at him in disbelief.

He quickly scrambled to his desk saying, "I know. I know. Take my seat and be quiet."

It was very hard for David to take a seat and be quiet. According to his medical and social history, his mother fed a daily drug habit during her pregnancy. As a consequence of this, he was born addicted to heroin. After medical withdrawal was successful, he was released from the hospital into the care of his grandmother.

As a result of this traumatic beginning and the instability in his present-day environment, he had very poor self-image and very little self-control. He was moved around from relative to relative—whoever would take him for a while. No one wanted him for long. He had even spent one school year in residential care for emotionally-disturbed children because he had been expelled from a public school due to his "out-of-control behavior."

I said, "Oh, no, David. No, I don't want you to stop singing. I didn't even know you could sing. That was wonderful. You sound so much like James Ingram. No, David, don't stop singing. Please sing that same song again in its entirety."

"Alright, then," he said. He was now looking at me in disbelief. He paused for a moment before pulling himself up so he stood straight and tall; then he began:

> I did my best, but I guess my best wasn't good enough
> 'Cause here we are back where we were before.
> Seems nothing ever changes
> We're back to being strangers
> Wondering if we ought to stay or head on out the door . . .

His voice was so powerful for a fourteen-year-old; he seemed transformed. He was transformed. He was an artist giving his best.

I felt my eyes begin to sting. The other students were transfixed as they gazed upon this uncontrollable boy who was in complete control of his voice and his composure.

He stirred up some magic in the air of the old mobile unit. He enunciated carefully as he rang out each word with just the right amount of volume, the right amount of pause, the right amount of feeling.

At times, he would close his eyes and move his hands in rhythm with his words.

> . . . Just Once
> Can we figure out, what we keep doing wrong
> Why the good times never last for very long?
> Where are we going wrong?
> Just once can't we find a way to finally make it right?
> To make the magic last for more than just one night
> I know we could, break thru it
> If we could just get to it . . .

The students began quietly swaying from side to side in their desks as he continued:

> Just once I want to understand
> Why it always comes back to goodbye
> Why can't we get ourselves in hand
> And admit to one another
> We're no good without each other
> Take the best and make it better
> Find a way to stay together
> Just once. We can get to it—
> Just once.[1]

When he finished—much too soon—the children and I all applauded simultaneously. This boy, who seemingly had no attributes to praise, was receiving compliments from all of us. Squeals and whistles erupted.

He bowed. He was beaming and smiling. He was remarkably calm. I had never seen him so much at ease. His gleaming teeth shone beneath that not-often-seen smile. He was happy! He was radiant! He had done something grand that was appreciated by others.

It didn't happen often enough to this misplaced boy, but it did happen today. He will remember.

Just once, he broke through it.

He did his best and it was good enough.

"Celebrate the Power of Great Music."

—James Ingram

---

1   Ingram, J., *The Power of Great Music* CD. (USA: Warner Bros. Records Inc., 1991)

III. The School Psychologist

"See that you do not despise one of these little ones . . ."

—Matthew 18:10 (RSV)

Little Spider Boy

I do not know his name. A frantic teacher brought him to me saying, "He's been crying all morning. He thinks his grandmother is going to die."

He sat in a chair in the corner of this dingy room, which served as the Counseling Center on the days that I, the itinerant psychologist, was in this school. There was not even a window in this make-shift, closet-of-a-room. How badly this room needed to emit cheerfulness, even if it could not evoke it.

His small brown head with its closely-cropped hair sat atop a skinny trunk of a body. His small arms and legs dangled lifelessly from this tiny stem. He did not look up at me as his teacher left us alone. Quietly, he sat now.

Perhaps, I will see him always in my visual memory. How can I erase this indelible, lanky spider-of-a-boy perched pitifully in the dark corner of a room, awaiting a vehicle to bear his pain?

I do not possess, nor do I believe there is, adequate training available that enables one to say, in poignant moments such as this, the right thing. He did not move.

I rolled slowly forward in my chair close enough to reach out and gently touch a knee of one spiny spider leg. "Touch," Helen Keller had said, "can be more reaffirming than words." I touched because I could not speak.

He looked up at me and began crying anew. I embraced him as one instinctively does a crying child. I held that frail, bony body, wondering how it could possibly house such massive sobs. I estimated that he was about nine or ten years of age—not by his appearance—but by the grade-level assignment of the teacher who had brought him to me.

When he began talking, I learned—as is often the case—that today's presenting problem was not the underlying pain of this child.

True, his grandmother was ill and in the hospital, and he was worried. True, there was no one else to watch over him and his little brother in her absence. True, this was the precipitating problem.

But, the imposing story, more piercing, included tales of raw violence and harsh, repellent scenes that began as far back as his memory would take him.

He was only six years old when he witnessed his mother murder his father. "She stabbed him over and over with a butcher knife. He was moaning and hollering; blood was going everywhere. I couldn't do nothing."

"But," he quickly adds, "he was mean to her."

His mother, now serving a prison term, is seldom seen. He and his younger brother reside with their aging grandmother, who is now critically ill, in a neighborhood marked in this town by poverty and crime. There is no grandfather in the home.

What feeble attempts of comfort can I offer this child? I lament my own inadequacy as I bewail his deplorable existence. I think of concrete, immediate things I can do: call the hospital, try to check on his grandmother. Call the Department of Social Services to investigate provisional or permanent care. See that the principal of the school is aware of his plight.

I do not want to call; I do not want to check. I want to take this remarkable child who speaks softly of his dream to do well in school so he can become a doctor—or maybe a policeman—home with me. I want to take him into my home as quickly as I had taken him into my heart in this eternity of time.

I do not want to leave him engulfed in social quicksand that could drag him, without mercy, down into an inconsolable stance. I do not want him to become a permanent spider boy, gangling from a chair in a dark room embedded in abandonment.

And, yet, I know that he must leave in a short while because another child is always waiting—another quivering child who is waiting for hope. How inadequate are we when we must try to harness the irretrievable brightness of a child's hope in the dark corners of our dingy, make-shift adult worlds?

"And in the naked night I saw
Ten thousand people, maybe more,
People talking without speaking,
People hearing without listening."

—Paul Simon, *The Sounds of Silence*

Rusty's Glasses

When entering a teacher's classroom, I do not knock on the door. A knock on the door would disturb the children and take their attention away from their task at hand. I have great respect for what goes on in a classroom. I have been there myself and I know what it takes to manage, instruct, and motivate a group of diverse children. I have great respect, too, for effective teachers who can accomplish this. I certainly do not want to intrude. In my tenure as a school psychologist, I have observed some teachers who are so outstanding and enjoyable that I hate to remove the referred child from the magic abound in their classroom.

I try to slip in as quietly and as inconspicuously as possible. I am delighted when I see a small table and chair located in the back of the room where I may sit unnoticed. The teacher, of course, knows which students I am there to observe and is expecting me. The children, more often than not, know I am the school psychologist, but, of course, do not know who it is I came to observe. It always amuses me when a child (always a boy) will hastily point his finger at himself and shake his head up and down with that questioning look on his face that asks, "Is it me?" I always quickly shake my head "no" in response and look away so that the child can get back to work.

When I go to observe a child in his/her classroom I have already studied the file compiled by parents, teachers, social workers, and school nurses, which contains the child's medical and social history, as well as his school achievement and a measured scale of his adaptive behavior. I know the child's name, but do not know which child it is. The alert teacher will call enough students by name as he or she continues with the lesson so I may be able to identify the child. But today, it was not necessary that his name be called.

Rusty's history indicates that he has a vision problem that could be corrected with glasses. Reading that information on paper did not produce the same effect as seeing it in person. The teacher had several math problems on the board, which the children were to copy and complete for homework. (Perhaps I should interject here that this was before the onset of smart boards, laptops, tablets, and other electronic devices that are now being utilized in classrooms.) Teachers were still depending on the long-reliable blackboard.

There was one little fellow in this class of third graders whose desk was pushed extremely close to the board. It had to be Rusty.

When all had finished copying the math problems, they moved their chairs into a circle around the teacher. She was reading them a story about foxes. They were to answer her oral questions as posed. This activity, I believe, was designed to practice their listening skills as well as their comprehension skills. Sometimes, a few would wave their hands in anticipation of her questions. Rusty was one who did that often. He was so engaged in the story that sometimes he would even jump up from his chair to declare his answer. I loved his enthusiasm and the fact that he could answer correctly all the questions posed.

As indicated by his academic history, Rusty has a reading problem and difficulty completing written work. It was suspected that this was largely due to his vision problem. From what I had observed thus far, I tended to agree with that supposition. I could hardly wait to attend to him myself and get a measure of his intelligence—hoping to validate that notion.

At a break in the lessons presented, the teacher brought him to me in the back of the room. I said, "That was a great story about foxes, wasn't it, Rusty?"

"Yes," he agreed. "It was a great story." He had on overalls and a blue checkered shirt. His little muddy cowboy boots looked as if he had been running livestock. His short-cropped hair was so bright red that it looked almost orange—and he never stopped smiling.

As we were walking down the hall together toward the testing room I said, "Rusty, you are going to love this: We have foxes, raccoons, squirrels, deer, and rabbits that come into our backyard."

"You do!" He said with amazement.

"And listen to this," I continued. "We leave cookies out for the raccoons, and we throw slices of bread on the ground for the foxes.

Sometimes, my husband holds the bread in his hand at arm's length trying to coax the foxes to come closer. They have gotten close, but have not yet come close enough to take the bread from his hand."

"Wow!" he exclaimed. "How many?"

"Well," I said, knowing now that we were definitely friends, "we have counted two red foxes, three fat raccoons, and lots of little squirrels. The deer are usually in groups of four or five. We live in the country and our yard is surrounded by woods. Oh, yes, and we also have a pond where Canadian geese, mallards, and wood ducks drop by for a quick swim."

His little, adorable face was aglow and I knew there was no doubt that I loved him. How I wished I could take him home with me so he could see for himself. But then I was brought back to the problem at hand—his impaired vision would not allow him to see very far into the distance.

"Do you have cooters in that pond?" he asked.

"Sure. But my husband does not like those cooters. He says they will eat the fish. He wants to get rid of those cooters."

"Did you know you can make some good cooter stew out of them cooters?" he asked.

"No, I didn't. Tell me about that."

I could see that he was happy to add something to my animal story. So eager was he to tell me something that I did not know.

"Well, my grandpa can make the best cooter stew you ever tasted," he proudly reported.

"Wow!" I said to show my appreciation for his addition to the story.

I knew from his social history that he was being raised by his grandparents in a low socio-economic environment. His single mother was in and out of the house and his life. She had been made aware of his vision problem by the school's nurse (more than once) and had promised to get his much-needed glasses (more than once). But, as of yet, she had not done so. (It was believed that his grandparents could not afford the cost of an optical examination and the necessary glasses.)

Later at home that day, I was at the sink scraping carrots preparing our supper. Our two daughters were now away at college and it was just my husband and me. I began to tell him the story of Rusty.

And then it happened. I had no warning; I was not aware that it was coming. In the middle of my story, I just burst into sobs. I could not harness these uncontrollable sobs as I thought of that little boy who so loved life and deserved to see it in all its glory. "If he were my little boy, he would have some glasses," I managed to say.

My husband, no doubt touched by the story himself, reached for me and as my head rested on his shoulder, he said, "Don't cry. We will get him some glasses. We will get him some glasses. Go back tomorrow and tell them we will get him some glasses."

"Yes, yes, I will," I said. Yet, even while saying that I knew I faced a dilemma or two.

My first dilemma was that I was too emotionally involved. I knew, professionally, I should not allow myself to get so attached to these children. It could possibly cloud my objectivity and perhaps interfere with my ability to make an appropriate diagnosis.

The second dilemma I had to face was the fact that I was angry at his mother for her neglect of this wondrous child. And if I were to see that he got his glasses, that would further reinforce the neglect. She would continue to relinquish the care of her own child to those who would do it for her as she had done with his grandparents.

The next morning, upon my arrival at the school, the first thing I did was to go in to see the principal. I had met him, but knew little about him. He listened carefully to me as I relayed my entire story. He then told me that before he became a principal, he was a director of special services. When I learned that, my spirits lifted. Directors of special services are the ones in charge of all special education programs in their districts. Therefore, he would have knowledge and understanding of the special-needs child. (Remember the principal who said that Sadie was "mean as hell"?) Well, I did not expect to hear such from this man.

Nor did I.

Even though he agreed with my two stated dilemmas, he went beyond that to offer these comforting words: "Don't worry, Mrs.

Evans. I have already contacted the Lions' Club and they are going to provide Rusty with the glasses he needs."

I wanted to jump right up and give him a big, grateful hug, but acting more sensibly, I extended my hand. "Thank you, sir." I said. "Thank you."

Rusty's intelligence, as tested, was within the normal range. With corrective lenses, his reading ability and written work improved notably. All he needed was a pair of glasses.

Now his enthusiasm for life and learning is matched with visual acuity that allows him to see all things more clearly—especially those foxes and cooters.

All he needed was a pair of glasses.

"Jesus said, 'Anyone who will not receive the kingdom of God like a little child will never enter it.'"

—Mark 10:15 (NIV)

WHAT TIME IS IT?

Most classroom teachers can identify early on those students who are exhibiting academic difficulty or behavioral problems. Before such a student is referred for a complete psycho-educational evaluation, the attending teacher must give written reports of different strategies or methods that he or she had used to try to remediate the identified problem. The identified problem, or target behavior, must be clearly stated in objective, measurable terms.

It is only after these attempted strategies have failed to bring about success will the child be referred to the school psychologist for further testing and assessment. This assessment will include a psychological and psycho-educational evaluation. Many students who experience academic problems may have psychological, social, or physiological problems as well. It is important to determine which of these problems is the underlying (primary) one and which is a resulting (secondary) one.

For example, a child with learning problems may also suffer emotionally. Does the learning problem bring about the emotional disturbance? Or, is the emotional disturbance causing the learning problems?

Through consultation, observation, and assessment, the psychologist attempts to determine the primary problem. We must—as accurately as possible—identify the underlying problem before we can attempt to adequately address it. We must consider the physical, the cognitive, the affective, and the behavioral domains before appropriate intervention can be initiated. Students can experience significant excesses or deficits in any, or all, of the domains.

Once all the assessment data have been collected, it becomes the psychologist's task to analyze and interpret the data before a psychological-educational diagnosis can be made. After which, comes recommendations for educational placement and/or intervention.

The assessment data include the child's social and medical history as obtained and compiled by the school social worker and the school nurse; observations and adaptive behavior rating scales of the child completed by both teachers and parents; my interview and systematic observations of the child in at least two different school settings; my academic achievement assessment (through standardized achievement test scores); and my assessment of the child's current level of functioning (through standardized IQ test scores).

Achievement test scores and intelligence test scores of the child are compared with the national test-score norms of other children of the same age and/or grade placement.

This process is extremely tedious and challenging. I like it particularly because it is detailed and challenging; it is never dull. I like it because it is extremely important. Each time I meet with a student, I am dealing with his or her well-being, his or her educational placement, and quite possibly—his or her future.

Each time, I consider it a responsible privilege, and I am thankful for the opportunity.

After all the preliminary due process work has been completed, it is time for me (and you) to meet Justin.

Justin is a scrawny, pale five-year-old kindergarten child. He has no distinguishing qualities making him the kind of child one could easily overlook. The two times that I observed him, I never saw him smile. His almost colorless eyes darted anxiously around the room; yet, he seemed to be detached from all classroom activity. He constantly rubbed across the top of his short-cut ashen hair. He put his head down on his desk—as if in exasperation—four times during one thirty-minute observation period. No one spoke to him except to give him directions. He made no attempt to interact with others. He would do as he was told without showing any emotion. He allowed others—children and teachers alike—to direct him.

When I went to his classroom to take him to our testing room he came without comment. My impression thus far, based on my observations of him, is that he is an overly-controlled child. I surmise

that he possibly lives with very authoritarian adults. He may have suf-
fered both verbal and physical abuse. But these were only specula-
tions, not facts. Nevertheless, guided by the experience of working
with children, one becomes more mindful of that which is not spoken.
Non-verbal behavior speaks loudly.

At first, I tried to engage him in casual conversation, but he
would have none of it. So, I explained to him as gently as I knew how
why he was with me and what we were about to do.

"I'm going to ask you a few questions, Justin, and I want you
to answer as best you can. You will not know all the answers, and that
is okay. Just answer what you can. Are you ready for me to start?"

He replied with a question of his own—the first time he had
spoken. "What time is it?"

Rather an unusual question I thought, but, I told him the time:
It was 9:35 in the morning.

His classroom teacher had thought him to be mentally-retarded, so I began with questions below that of his age group even though
I did not believe him to be mentally-retarded. At the same time, I
have to bear in mind that his teacher has spent more time with him
than have I; therefore, I must allow for her judgment. He was able
to answer an adequate number of questions from a scale designed to
measure the intellectual functioning of children between the ages of
two-and-a-half and four-and-a-half, even though he appeared preoc-
cupied with thoughts of his own.

As I was beginning the scale of questions for a five-year-old,
he asked again, "What time is it?"

I said, "It is now nine-fifty-eight," and continued with the academic achievement questions for his age group. He was fidgety; he
was rubbing the top of his head and rocking in his chair. I could see
that he was distressed, but I had to administer the required tests before
I could make recommendations for his educational intervention and
correct placement.

The third time he asked me about the time, it was 10:15.

"Is it 10:00 yet?" he asked.

I stopped the test. I closed the book and said, "Justin, 10:00
has passed. What makes you so concerned about the time?"

His reply stung me. "We have snack time at 10:00 every day, and now I've missed it because I am here."

He got up from his desk and began pacing back and forth across the floor rubbing his head. "I missed snack time. I missed snack time."

I was finally beginning to understand his concern. "Justin," I said gently. "Stop pacing and talk to me. What did you have to eat before you came to school this morning?"

"Nothing," he replied.

"Did you not have breakfast at school?" I asked.

"No, our bus was late and we had to go straight to class."

"Alright then," I continued. "What did you have to eat last night before you went to bed?"

"Nothing," he replied.

Oh my God, it's true, I thought. *This child is hungry.* Of course, he's hungry; he's undernourished. Much like a pacing animal, he is in pursuit of food.

A psychologist, teacher, coach—anyone who is trying to get the best performance a child has to offer—cannot get it from a child who is hungry. Surely, Abraham Maslow taught us that!

I reached my hand out to Justin. "Come with me, Justin," I said. "I will see that you don't miss your snack time."

"It's already over!" he tearfully declared.

"We'll find another way. Come with me."

We went straight to the principal's office. Perhaps a male principal could have handled the situation as well as she did, but I was grateful for her. She was a lovely young woman who listened intently to me as I said, "I cannot test this child until he has something to eat; he's extremely hungry."

Immediately, she put a comforting arm on his frail, little shoulder and said, "Come with me, Justin. Let's see if we can't find you some breakfast."

He smiled. It was the first time I had ever seen him smile.

I believe Justin's primary problem is an environmentally-induced one. Again, as Maslow taught us: one cannot attend to higher-level aspirations until lower-level needs are met[1]. Biological needs are primary; safety needs are essential. These needs must be met before one is motivated to achieve higher-level needs such as attending to learning tasks.

No, Justin is not mentally-retarded. He is malnourished, mistreated, and misunderstood.

It is up to us in the school environment to see that his needs are met as best we can. This will involve an interdisciplinary team working together: principal, regular classroom teacher, special-needs teacher, social worker, counselor, school nurse, and school psychologist.

Yes, this group of well-trained professionals will work together for the sake of this one child, as we so often do. But, we will accomplish little without the inclusion and cooperation of Justin's parents. We have too often seen much of our dedicated work undermined and overpowered by uncaring parents.

It is true that "Home is where your story begins." To that, I would sadly add this message: "Home is where carefully-planned school interventions can end if no one there seems to care."

"So it is not the will of my Father who is in heaven that one of these little ones should perish."

—Matthew 18:14 (RSV)

---

1   Maslow, A. H., *Motivation and Personality* (New York: Harper & Row, 1954)

WHO'S EMOTIONALLY DISTURBED?

Tobias had been referred by his teacher for psychological testing. According to her, he was out of control due to his emotional disturbance. Again, all preliminary work had been completed before I went into the classroom to observe him. And did I learn a lot by doing so.

As I walked into the room, I saw that the teacher had the entire class of fifth graders lined up against the wall. As she called each child's name, that child was to come to her desk where she would then try to give the student some individual attention concerning some work that had been assigned.

I knew immediately that this was not a good idea. Individual attention is, of course, a good idea. But lining up twenty-five fifth graders against the wall in hopes that they will wait quietly for their name to be called is an unrealistic expectation. And it certainly was not working.

She spent more time yelling at the waiting students than she did attending to the individual student seated near her. Her threats were not working, yet she continued this menagerie as if in time it would become effective. I had been in the classroom for seventeen minutes. During that time, she had called only three students to her desk. After her individual consultation with students, they, in turn, were then expected to go to their seats and sit quietly without any further assignment being given to them.

My attention was drawn to a slim, lively boy who seemed to be in charge of the line. He would turn to those behind him and make snide comments in response to her rambling threats. Snickers and giggles coming from the other students would then burst forth. They were not only ignoring her idle threats, but such threats had become an object of their amusement.

Of course, they were being disrespectful to their teacher, and that behavior should stop. Yet, I know that teachers who have earned respect will not be treated disrespectfully. And those who have not earned respect will continue to suffer at the hands of their students.

Such as this reminds me—contrary to what some may think—effective teaching is neither for the faint-hearted nor the lazy. It is for the bold, the undaunted, the creative, the caring.

Once the boy in charge of the line said to the others, "Let's all sit on the floor," they did so without question. She made no comment, no attempt, to correct that behavior.

I had no doubt that this boy was the one whom she had referred for testing. Clearly, she could not control him. In addition, he seemed to have more control over the students than she did. In this situation, I had little sympathy for her.

If one cannot manage a class, one cannot teach that class. All would-be teachers should be required to take a course in classroom management. Regardless of her personal story, regardless of her other excuses, she should not be in a classroom if she is not able to control herself and the students under her care. I had more sympathy for the students than I did for her.

In every profession we find those who are exemplary—those who bring credit to their profession. We also find those who are objectionable. I have found one today. With her ranting and threatening, she not only brings dishonor to our profession, she also may instill a dislike for learning in our students.

It doesn't take a school psychologist to realize that leaders and/or troublemakers in a classroom can be helpful. Identifying them is easy; they emerge on their own—early. The behavior of their peers toward them is also a good indicator of how much influence they can exert in a classroom. It is essential that teachers work to establish a relationship with these class leaders and/or troublemakers based on mutual respect. This may not be an easy task, but it will prove worthwhile as teachers direct misguided energies into more productive and rewarding pursuits. Once the leaders and/or troublemakers are under control, the rest of the class will usually follow accordingly.

When the bell rang to dismiss the class, she had called only eight students to her desk. As the students scurried out the door, I thought of all the valuable class time that was wasted rather than re-directed.

I went forward to speak to her. She was obviously distraught.

I introduced myself as graciously as I could. Not surprising, she was as hostile to me as she had been with the students.

"I hope you can see how awful they are—especially that Tobias," she declared.

"I will be glad to help you manage Tobias and your class if you would allow me," I offered.

"What could you do?" she almost sneered.

"I can give you some techniques for behavior management that have been proven to work and—"

She did not let me finish. "Oh, no," she said. "I have heard about that behavior modification stuff, and I don't believe in it. No thank you." She began gathering her papers as if we were through talking.

Okay, I said to myself. *Let's just be honest and forthright.* To her, I said, "That young boy, Tobias, the one you referred for psychological testing, has more control over your class than you do. Once you employ more effective management techniques and methods of teaching, you can better establish and maintain control. I will be glad to help you; I want to help you. But I can only offer; I cannot force you to accept."

She left me then. Without another word, she turned and left me standing alone in her room.

I attached my behavior observation of Tobias to her referral form of him. I also stated that, in my professional opinion, the disrespect shown her by the students could be eliminated—or at least decreased—with appropriate and systematic behavior management strategies and more effective instructional methods. In addition, I stated that I had offered to help her establish a behavior management program, but she had refused my help.

I personally took a copy of this to the principal. While in his presence, I also told him that, in my opinion, the teacher was more emotionally-disturbed than the student she referred.

Weeks later, I learned that some time after that day, she had resigned from teaching.

I would hope that in her absence, she is replaced by a caring, well-trained, calm teacher who comes well-armed with successful strategies of classroom management.

One who recognizes that creative, well-planned instructional methods that motivate and inspire will eliminate a host of would-be discipline problems.

Such teachers are out there; I have seen them. I know them. And, yes, they love what they do and it shows.

My concern for this particular teacher, however, is minimal.

Working as a school psychologist, I am—as always—an advocate for the child.

"It is human to err; it is devilish to remain willfully in error."

—St. Augustine

Pathological Encopresis?

Public law 94-142, the Education for All Handicapped Children Act of 1975, and its successor, the Individuals with Disabilities Education Act (IDEA) of 1992, include all children with disabilities from infancy to age twenty-one.

This mandates, among other sanctions, that each child who has been placed in a special education program be re-evaluated every three years. The law is clear that each pupil must be educated in the least restrictive environment. Thus, re-evaluation is necessary to ensure that all children are educated in an environment that best fits their needs. With effective intervention, those needs may change from year to year.

Trained and certified, by both state and national standards, school psychologists are the only ones in a school system who are authorized to complete psycho-educational evaluations and make recommendations for educational intervention and placement. Therefore, school psychologists are very busy in that they have many students to re-evaluate each year, as well as provide due process to all new students who have been referred for psycho-educational evaluation.

Sometimes, however, issues may arise in the regular classroom that call upon the school psychologist to investigate matters without an actual referral being set in stone.

Such was the case with Levi.

The first time Levi, a six-year-old first grader, soiled his pants, his teacher treated it as an involuntary occurrence. She realized, of course, that sometimes young children have upset stomachs and cannot control bowel emission. Or, it may be that they are too embarrassed to ask to be excused to the restroom. She took him to the principal's office and the school got in touch with his mother. His mother, a single parent who lived within walking distance of the school, brought him clean clothes.

Meanwhile, the principal had asked the male physical education teacher to take him to the gym and allow him to shower so that he would be clean when his fresh clothes arrived.

The second time it happened they all went through the same process again. But by the third time it happened, I was asked to investigate.

I first met with his teacher. She was an experienced teacher with a reputation for effectiveness. Her message to me emphasized that she was not trained to deal with such matters. In addition, it was disturbing her entire class—not only by the foul odor emitted in the classroom—but also by the interruption of having him taken out and returned each time. It was, she insisted, disturbing to all the other children and not fair to them. I understood her position and agreed. I inquired as to his learning ability and she reported that he was able to follow instructions and complete all tasks required of a first-grader. That helpful information eliminated any evidence of mental retardation.

Later, the teacher, the principal, and I met with the mother. She declared that Levi was not in the habit of doing this and she did not understand why it was happening. He did not have any anatomical defects that would cause this. Nor, according to her, was it a lack of proper training. Ruling out any organic defects, or mental retardation, or a lack of training, it appeared to be neurotic soiling.

Oftentimes, psychologists and therapists go rapidly into a search for psychopathology when a child is manifesting behaviors that are abnormal.

Encopresis, or fecal-soiling, is certainly abnormal behavior.

However, I, being more of a cognitive-behaviorist than a psychoanalyst, will first look for antecedents and consequences of a behavior. This helps me to better understand what is causing and maintaining the target behavior. It was curious to me as to why this behavior had just begun to manifest itself. Something was causing a new, inappropriate behavior to appear.

It was time to interview the child. Upon entering the room where I was to spend time with him, Levi appeared a little afraid. My first task, as always, was to quickly develop rapport and put the child at ease. After some time of talking about his cool sneakers and what he liked to do for fun, I asked him if he realized that soiling his clothes was not a good thing to do. He nodded in agreement.

I began trying to identify antecedents for his soiling behavior.

"What happens," I asked, "right before you soil your clothes? Do you have a stomach ache or a sick feeling?"

"The first time I had a stomach ache, but the other times, I didn't," he replied.

I continued. "The other times when you did not have a stomach ache and you soiled yourself, did something happen in the classroom to upset you?"

"No," he replied, "I just did it."

"You did it even though you knew that it was not a good thing to do?"

"Yes," he said.

Perhaps, I thought, there may be some psychopathology involved, but I also thought it important to consider the consequences of his behavior. Behavior that is not reinforced will tend to extinguish. B. F. Skinner proved this in his laboratory with rats and pigeons.[1] I have evidence of that myself in my practice—both in and out of the classroom.

I considered what happened each time after he had soiled himself:

* He got to leave the classroom, which could be reinforcing.

* He got to spend time with Mr. Morris, which could also be reinforcing.

* Mr. Morris was the only male he would have contact with during the entire school day.

*In addition, Mr. Morris, being a friendly and congenial man, would have been careful not to embarrass Levi.

* He got to take a shower.

Could these consequences be maintaining and reinforcing his soiling behavior? Yes, I believed all that was worth further investigating.

"Levi," I asked, "do you like Mr. Morris?"

"Yes," he replied, "I like Mr. Morris. He's nice."

---

1   Skinner, B. F., *A Matter of Consequences* (New York: Knopf, 1983)

"Well, how do you feel about having to take a shower each time you soil yourself?"

"I love the shower," he gleefully replied. "I have never had a shower before. We don't have a shower at my house. It's fun with the water running over my head and down my body. I love splashing around in it. I love going to the shower."

"How do you take a bath at home?" I asked him.

"I take a bath from a dishpan in the kitchen. We don't have a shower and our bathtub is stopped up. The water don't run out."

Well, now we are getting somewhere, I thought. The first time he soiled himself, it was most likely an accident. But since the shower was so rewarding, he thought he would continue to soil himself just to go have a fun shower and spend time with Mr. Morris.

I hated to take the shower experience away from him since he found it so rewarding, so I had to use that rewarding experience in a way to reinforce appropriate behavior—which, in this case, was non-soiling—rather than allowing it to maintain the inappropriate behavior of soiling.

I developed a quick plan: "Levi," I began. "Mr. Morris, the P.E. teacher can no longer allow you to take a shower if you soil your pants."

"He can't? Why not?" He began to whimper.

"Because, Levi, there has been a change. Mr. Morris will allow you to take a shower on Wednesdays and Fridays only at the end of the school day. And you will take a shower on those days only if you have gone the preceding days without soiling your clothes."

He looked confused.

"Let me go over it again," I said to him, slower this time. "Now listen carefully. If you go Monday, Tuesday, and Wednesday without soiling your clothes, Mr. Morris will let you have a shower before the end of the school day on Wednesday. Then, if you go without soiling your clothes on Thursday and Friday, Mr. Morris will let you have a shower before the end of the school day on Friday. Now, if you soil your clothes, we will call your mother to come get you without Mr. Morris giving you a shower. That means you will have to leave the classroom and sit in the principal's office in your soiled pants until your mother gets here. Do you understand?"

He nodded that he did understand, but I still was not sure. "I will explain this to your mother and to your teacher, and to Mr. Morris so that they will agree to it and help you to remember."

"But, really, Levi, the only thing you have to remember is that if you want to have a shower near the end of the school day, you must not soil your pants. And, you will not be taken out of class anymore. You will have your shower toward the end of the school day."

I am pleased to say—with the cooperation of Levi's teacher, his mother, the principal, and Mr. Morris—the plan worked.

I am also pleased to say that when trying to figure out a practical solution to a disturbing problem, common sense can still prevail.

"It is common sense to take a method and try it."

—FDR

TERRELL: "HE'S WILD"

Terrell is a seven-year-old, first-grade repeater. He comes to this elementary school in the middle of the year from a coastal island school outside our district. He comes with a diagnosis of EMH (Educable Mentally Retarded).

When a special needs child comes into our schools, we always review the records from his previous school, including the psychological diagnosis and recommendations. In addition, we conduct further testing to ensure that his placement is correct. Terrell's records indicate that he has been in a resource room for the mildly-retarded—meeting that class once a day. Other times during the day, he was mainstreamed into regular classrooms.

However, it doesn't take long for his first-grade teacher to demand that he be taken out of her classroom and placed in a self-contained class for EMH children because "he is wild."

Describing a child as "wild" is a general description that connotes a great deal, but it is not an acceptable description because the target behaviors must be stated specifically. Upon my request, I received the following specific behaviors from his teacher:

> *He crawls around on the floor under the tables.*
> *He frightens other children by grabbing them and hugging them.*
> *He makes animal noises.*
> *He is not clean.*
> *He does not stay in his seat.*
> *He does not follow directions.*
> *He runs around the room.*
> *He does not know colors or numbers.*
> *He cannot print his name—or spell it.*
> *He is non-compliant and becomes defiant when punished.*
> *It's hard to understand what he says; I think he speaks Gullah.*
> *Sometimes he goes to sleep on the floor and I do not wake him.*

In my first interview session with Terrell, I learned much about him. (I could make up these stories, but the truth goes beyond my imagination.)

"Why you git me in here? I not do noth'in."

"I just thought I would like to get to know you better since you are a new student in our school," I offered.

I put some Transformer toys from my bag onto the table. He picked one up with interest.

"What do you do after school, Terrell?" I asked him as he took the Transformer apart.

"Well, the furs thang I do is go git de wadder."

"Tell me about getting the water."

"I hav'eh git it from de streem."

"Where is the stream?"

"It be behin de house. I hav'eh git three bukets full."

"You go to the stream three times to get a bucket of water each time. Is that right?"

"Yah, dat's right."

"Is there no one to help you get the water?"

"No. Just me and Grandma. She blind."

"Just you and your grandmother live in your house and she cannot see. Is that right?"

"Yah, dat's right. She see a lil'le bit, but not much. My un'cle, he come sometime. But un'cle not come much."

"Well, you are such a big boy to help your grandmother like that."

"I hav'eh help her. She got nobody but me."

"What are some other things you do to help your grandmother?"

"I hav'eh put de ke'sene in de het'er when it be cold."

"Where is the heater located?"

"In de middle of the floor."

"You put the kerosene in a heater that sits in the middle of the floor."

"Yah, dat's right. Can I keep these here transforms?"

"Yes, you may keep them."

"I kin take 'em home wid me?"

"Yes, you may take them home with you. Where do you live, Terrell?"

"My house be in a trail pak."

"Do you know the name of that trailer park where you live?"

"No. No nam. Dis transform don't work."

"Yes, it does. Turn it around and try again."

"Tell me some other interesting things about you, Terrell." He seemed to like the attention I was giving him.

"You see dis here place on my han?" He displayed it with pride. "A mus'rat bit me."

"A muskrat bit you on your hand?"

"Yah, I kilt him. I beat him wit de broom and kilt him. My grandma say, 'Trel, what you doin' over thar?'"

"I say, 'I kilt a mus'rat, Grandma. I beat him with the broom.' My grandma lauf and lauf. Sometime I kilt de roaches, too. They try cral in my ears and nose when I sleepin'."

I felt exhausted. Trying not to show my despair, I watched as Terrell turned the Transformers around and sat them together in a straight line.

I asked him, "What is your uncle's name—the one who comes now and then?"

"He name be Smokey; that all I know—just Smokey."

"What does Smokey do when he comes to see you?"

"He drink a lotta beer and smok weed. He bring his gir'frien and I see em git naked."

I was feeling sick. This child is living in danger. Of course, I would see that our school social worker visit the home. The address would be on record in the office. I would give her the information I had collected today. I am sure that she would notify the Department of Social Services to further investigate the living conditions. We cannot allow him to continue to live in such peril. I would hope that the Department of Social Services would assign a worker to check this family's living situation on a regular basis and see that necessary and crucial improvements are made. However, I would not recommend that he be separated from his grandmother.

In order to better understand anyone, we must consider all aspects of his or her development. Sometimes, as in Terrell's case, the social environment in which he exists seems paramount in shaping his behavior.

How well, I ask, would any of us, living under theses conditions, appear "normal"?

It was not easy administering a test of intellectual functioning to Terrell. He could sit still and attend for only a few minutes without getting up and asking, "Wen we be don?"

After two sessions, I finally got an adequate sample. He scored in the mildly-retarded range. I felt that his score was affected by some non-intellectual factors such as motivation and, perhaps, even language.

My diagnosis was "cultural-familial mental retardation," which is a retardation due to psychological disadvantage. I recommended that he be placed in a self-contained EMH class for one school year, and that he be re-evaluated at the end of that time. Social skills training and academic remediation in a small group with a teacher trained to teach mildly-retarded children would be of great benefit to him. With appropriate intervention, he could be mainstreamed again.

Mental retardation is not measured only by low intelligence; it also refers to a failure in adaptive behavior. It is true that Terrell's classroom behavior is maladaptive. Yet, for a seven-year-old boy with adult responsibilities, no friends of his age to play with, living with and caring for a blind grandmother, and no positive adult role models to guide him, he has adapted well to his environment.

This is evidenced by his own words when referring to his situation and his grandmother:

"I hav'eh help her; she got nobody but me."

"If you would judge, understand."

—Lucius Annacus Seneca

Hiding Happiness

I sat across from eight-year-old Joshua searching his doleful, down-cast eyes. We had just completed the Wechsler Intelligence Scale for Children-Revised. He had scored within the low average range. The WISC-R is the instrument of choice in the assessment of intel-lectual functioning for school-aged children between the ages of six and sixteen-and-a-half years. "It calls upon a broad sampling of cognitive skills, requiring verbal and non-verbal skills, and in-volving several levels of abstraction."[1] Like all Wechsler scales, it is divided into a verbal scale, a performance (non-verbal) scale, and a full scale summary. It is quite valuable in evaluating the cur-rent intellectual functioning of school-aged children in under-standing their current performance and in suggesting alternatives for intervention.

I believed Joshua's scores on both scales to be depressed be-cause he exerted little effort. I tried as much as possible—within the framework of required standardization—to make the assessment in-teresting and appealing to him, but he never showed any interest.

My attention was called back to the social worker's descrip-tion of the family upon her visitation: *"Mother young, frail, taut and tense, fearful; father not present during the visit."*

After finishing the test, I pulled out of my briefcase a picture of a family. I often use such as this as a projective measure of sorts to find out as much as possible via conversation. I showed the picture to Joshua and asked him to describe what he saw.

"I see people," he replied.

"Do you think this could be a family?" I asked.

"Yes," he said.

---

1 Wechsler, D., *The Wechsler Intelligence Scale for Children-Revised* (New York: Psychological Corporation, 1974)

"Show me the dad." He pointed to the adult male reading the paper.

"Show me the mother." He pointed to the adult female sitting on the sofa sewing. There was also a little girl reading a book and a smaller boy with a dog.

"Do you think this could be your family?" I asked.

"No," he said. "I have never seen my daddy read the paper or my mama sew. It could be my sister though, because she reads all the time after she finishes her chores."

"Could that little boy be you?" I continued—glad that he was responding with some interest.

"No," he said. "I don't have a dog."

"Do you like dogs?" I asked him.

"Yes, but my daddy won't let me have one. He has hunting dogs in a pen, but we are not allowed to have pets."

He continued, "Once, for my birthday, my sister Joni bought me a goldfish, and a bowl, and a package of food for it. She cleaned my aunt's house and earned $3 each time. My mama can't drive and our aunt lives in a house down the dirt road from us, and sometimes she will take us places. She took my sister to Walmart and she bought me that for my birthday."

"What a nice thing for your sister to do."

"Yes, it made me so happy, but we had to hide it under the bed so our daddy wouldn't know. But he found it anyway. He stepped on the goldfish and killed it. He whipped us both for having it."

"What did you and Joni do after that?" I asked.

"Nothing. There was nothing we could do."

I felt sure that Joshua was showing the effects of learned helplessness. As research psychologist Martin Seligman pointed out, when oppressed people learn that their efforts have no effect on outcomes, they give up and quit trying.[2] Joshua, no doubt, is depressed and passive because he knows that nothing he does will help him escape the

---

2   Seligman, M. E., *Helplessness* (San Francisco: Freeman, 1975)

punishment rendered by his abusive father. This lack of self-determination spills over into other aspects of his life.

I thought it would be helpful to interview his sister, Joni. In talking with her teacher, I was told that she was a straight-A student. Her teacher said that she was very smart—highly-motivated to do well—and never caused any trouble. When I asked her about Joni's overall demeanor, she stated that she did not engage in interaction with the other students and appeared to be somewhat withdrawn. Yet, the students seemed to like her and often commented on her outstanding ability. They would say, "Ask Joni. I bet she knows the answer."

I found Joni to be much like the social worker had described her mother. She, too, was tiny, frail, and taut. Joni tells me that their father is very mean and that he whips them often. Her mother does not intervene when he whips them because he beats her, too. The mother cannot sign the papers for Joshua to receive special placement because the father will not allow it.

She also told me that one of Joshua's teachers had notified the school's guidance counselor when she noticed bruises on Joshua's arms and face. The guidance counselor then notified the Department of Social Services and someone was sent to their home to investigate. Her father told the social worker if anyone returned, he would shoot them. No one ever came back.

"I try to keep Joshua out of his way as much as possible," she said. "Our aunt, who lives down the road, will allow us to come over to her house and play sometimes."

Without placement, without intervention, what will become of Joshua? I can only speculate. Sometimes abused children continue to be withdrawn and internalize their fears and become more depressed and possibly suicidal. Such an environment also raises the possibility of nurturing an antisocial personality who externalizes his deep anger and fear onto others. Such children, knowing no happiness except the little they are able to hide, are broken-winged birds who will not be able to fly. Leading a normal life is out of their reach.

Joni, however, is smart and resilient enough that she may be able to save her brother. What an awesome task for a twelve-year-old little girl. Yet, she has been trying since she was four years old.

Perhaps this ignorant father (and I do not use that word

loosely) is not aware that domestic violence is a criminal offense. When the county sheriff comes calling and the agency for The Prevention of Child Abuse is notified, I doubt that he will, then, threaten to shoot anyone.

> **"All that is necessary for the triumph of evil
> is that good men do nothing."**
>
> **—Edmund Burke**

NATURE VS. NURTURE

Lonnie, an eleven-year-old male, was referred for psycho-educational assessment by his classroom teacher to determine his current levels of functioning and the appropriateness of his educational program and placement. Concerns noted included: *"Extreme inattentiveness, consistently failing grades, isolation from group, rarely focusing on tasks, and often not completing assigned work."*

According to the social information obtained by the school social worker, Lonnie lives at home with his adopted parents. Lonnie was adopted when he was seven years old; therefore, complete birth history is not available. His parents reported that they were told that Lonnie was malnourished at birth and showed a "failure to thrive."

Prior to being adopted, Lonnie lived in several foster homes and children's homes. According to the social worker, Lonnie's adopted parents are very loving and concerned about his well-being. They are willing to help Lonnie in any way possible, and they provide a very stable environment for him. He is presently under the care of Dr. J. Smith of Smith's Family Practice. Information obtained from Dr. Smith indicates "minimum brain dysfunction with resulting hyperactivity." No other medical problems are indicated.

His school records indicated that he received speech therapy during his first and second years at school. He repeated the first grade. There is no prior record of previous psycho-educational assessment or placement in special education classes. Vision and hearing were reported within normal limits by the school nurse. The speech clinician reported that his speech was currently within normal limits.

Upon observation of Lonnie in his fourth-grade classroom, I discovered him seated in the back of the room facing the teacher, near no other students. The class was involved in an English lesson, and the teacher was going over an assigned lesson orally with the class. Lonnie appeared to be working steadily and intently.

He writes with his left hand. He raised his right hand to volunteer a response one time during this observation period. He gave a correct response (one that required generating possibilities) and was reinforced socially by his teacher.

He showed signs of frustration when it appeared that his answers (on paper) did not correspond with oral responses given by his teacher and other students. Off-task behaviors consisted of looking around the room, biting his nails, and fidgeting in his desk. On-task behaviors included looking at his paper and book and responding to his teacher's question.

Lonnie raised his hand one time to volunteer an answer as compared to 90% of the class who raised their hands each time the teacher posed a question. Lonnie was well-groomed, appropriately-dressed, and pleasant looking, although he appeared to be smaller in stature than most of his male peers.

The most telling observation of Lonnie was made on the playground and in the cafeteria. On the playground, many of the children were engaged in group activities, but he did not approach them; nor was he invited to join. He was alone. There were no other children near him. He wandered around here and there. Although he was not mistreated, he was just ignored. Sometimes it appeared that he was muttering to himself.

In the lunchroom, too, he sat alone while eating his lunch. Non-acceptance by peers is the most striking observation I made of Lonnie. Acceptance by peers is an important factor in the social development of a middle-school child.

As he and I were walking to the room where I was to give the test, Lonnie conversed readily with me and appeared very motivated and interested in the possibility of being "tested." Although appearing a little fearful at first, he was polite and cooperative during the entire assessment and completed all tasks required of him. He responded well to my verbal encouragement. Once he declared, "I'm doing good on this test."

I responded, "Yes, you are doing good on this test."

I believe the results of my testing (aptitude and achievement), the behavior-rating scales completed by his teacher and parents, the social history obtained, and my observation of him in three different school settings are to be considered as a valid estimate of Lonnie's overall general aptitude for learning.

As a result of the overall evaluation, Lonnie is functioning within the low-average range of academic aptitude, the moderately-below average range of academic achievement, and the significantly-below average range in social behaviors.

The discrepancy between his cognitive ability and his current achievement and the significant discrepancy between his verbal IQ and his performance IQ as obtained through the WISC-R are consistent with the diagnosis of "learning disabled" and meet the state guidelines for placement. However, evidence of interfering emotional factors are also present as indicated by the Adaptive Behavior Scales completed by his teacher and parents and medical information given by his pediatrician, Dr. Smith.

The Adaptive Behavior Scale completed by his teacher indicates an inability to build satisfactory interpersonal relationships. All sub-scale scores and total behavior quotient fall within the significantly-below-average range. This must be kept in mind in the intervention programming.

I recommended that Lonnie be placed in a resource room for the learning disabled for one class period per day and mainstreamed in regular classes the remainder of the school day. Working with a certified teacher for the learning disabled, he could receive remedial assistance in his areas of weakness. I also recommended that social skills training and effective coping skills training be an important part of this intervention program.

Lonnie is a very fortunate child to be adopted by stable, loving parents. The question is: can a stable, healthy environment with good medical care and proper educational intervention compensate for a lack of proper prenatal care resulting in low birth weight and a "failure to thrive?" Certainly such an environment will make a difference, but the risk factors associated with low birth weight and failure to thrive will not be overcome easily—some will never be overcome entirely. It will require long-term effort on the part of all involved. That is the reason I believe family counseling (not provided by the school) would be beneficial to Lonnie and his family to fully understand their challenge.

Can the absence of an opportunity to build a trusting relationship from infancy prevent Lonnie from making such relationships now? According to Erik Erikson, a pioneer in child psychoanalysis, the most significant step in the social development of a newborn is having a basic trust of its environment.[1] Without supportive, nurturing, and loving attachment, trust will not be formed and mistrust will influence future relationships with other persons.

Human behavior results from both biological and environmental influences acting together. A wide variety of factors working together in a complex interaction of biological and social variables make us all what we are. The relative importance of each—for the most part—still remains a mystery.

Yet, it is clear that early deprivation disrupts cognitive development and slows physical development. One must consider the importance of both nature and nurture in all individuals. This is especially true when working with troubled children such as Lonnie.

Yes, Lonnie is fortunate to have loving parents who are providing him with opportunities to develop his potential in a nurturing environment.

To his parents—and to all those caring persons who are working with troubled children—I leave you with the inspiring words of American essayist and poet Ralph Waldo Emerson:

"To know that even one life has
breathed easier because you have lived;
this is to have succeeded."

---

[1] Erikson, E. H., *Childhood and Society* (2nd ed.) (New York: Norton, 1963)

Epilogue

The remnants I have shared with you are fragments of real children. I offer them as representative of the many I have served. Such distressed, troubled children can come from all socio-economic environments and all ethnic backgrounds. They can come from urban, rural, or suburban homes.

In today's diverse society, they may come bearing differences in culture, religion, race, or language. Nevertheless, they are all children and, amid their differences, they all hold one thing in common—a yearning for acceptance. They hunger for a sense of worthiness. They long for a chance to fly.

They are all ours.

Be alert. Be concerned. Be available.

"And Jesus took a child, and put him in the midst of them; and taking him in his arms, he said to them, 'Whoever receives one such child in my name receives me; and whoever receives me receives not me, but him who sent me.'"

—Mark 9:36-37 (RSV)

POST SCRIPT

Just a touch of humor added at the conclusion of my serious writing and your patient reading:

The psycho-educational program I conducted for emotionally-disturbed children in a public school setting (described in "The Mobile Unit" section of this book) was cited as an Exemplary Program for the Handicapped by our State Department of Education.

I was asked to give a report of my program to our local Board of Education. I was happy to do so since mine was the only such program operating in our school district and was selected, at that time, to be the model program for emotionally-handicapped public-school children throughout our state.

On the evening of my presentation to the board, it took a few moments for me to compose myself following the introduction I was given by the Director of Special Services in our district.

Rather than saying, "Our district's only teacher of the emotionally disturbed," she introduced me as "Our school district's only emotionally-disturbed teacher."

BIBLIOGRAPHY

Allen, J. *As a Man Thinketh.* USA: Barnes & Noble, Inc., 1992.

Arkoff, A. *The Illuminated Life.* University of Hawaii at Manoa: Allyn & Bacon, 1995.

Chernow, F. B. and C. Chernow. *Classroom Discipline and Control.* Parker Publishing Company, Inc., 1984.

Gallagher, J. *Teaching the Gifted Child* (2nd ed.) Allyn & Bacon, 1967.

Ellis, A. *Humanistic Psychotherapy: The Rational-Emotive Approach.* New York: McGraw-Hill, 1973.

Erikson, E. H. *Childhood and Society* (2nd ed.). New York: Norton, 1963.

Gibran, K. *Sand and Foam.* New York: Knopf, 1978.

———. *The Prophet,* (1975).

Hammill, D. and N. Bartel. *Teaching Children with Learning and Behavior Problems.* Allyn & Bacon, 1982.

Holy Bible. *Revised Standard Version.*

Ingram, J. Greatest Hits (1991). *The Power of Great Music* CD. USA: Warner Bros. Records Inc., 1991.

Maslow, A. H. *Motivation and Personality.* New York: Harper & Row, 1954.

———. *Toward a Psychology of Being* (2nd ed.) New York: Van Nos trand Reinhold Co., 1968.

May, R. *The Art of Counseling.* Abingdon Press, 1967.

Palladino, J. J., ed. *Abnormal Psychology Annual Editions* (2nd ed.) Dushkin/McGraw-Hill, 1998.

Reynolds, C. R., T. B. Gutkin, S. N. Elliott, and J. C. Witt. *School Psychology Essentials of Theory and Practice.* John Wiley & Sons, Inc., 1984.

Robinson, N. M. and H. B. Robinson. *The Mentally Retarded Child.* McGraw-Hill, 1976.

Schwartz, S. and J. H. Johnson. *Psychopathology of Childhood* (2nd ed.) Pergamon Press, 1985.

Seligman, M. E. *Helplessness.* San Francisco: Freeman, 1975.

Showman, McCowen, Biehler. *Psychology Applied to Teaching* (12th ed.) Houghton Mifflin Co., 2009.

Skinner, B. F. *A Matter of Consequences.* New York: Knopf, 1983.

Sprinthall, R. C., N. A. Sprinthall, and S. N. Oja. *Educational Psychology: A Developmental Approach* (7th ed.) McGraw-Hill, 1998.

Walton, D. *Emotional Intelligence: A Practical Guide.* MJF Books, 2012.

Webb, D., A. Metha, and F. Jordan. *Foundations of American Education* (5th ed.). Pearson, 2007.

Wechsler, D. *The Wechsler Intelligence Scale for Children—Revised.* New York: Psychological Corporation, 1974.

Wilson, G. T. and K. D. O'Leary. *Principles of Behavior Therapy.* Englewood Cliffs, NJ: Prentice-Hall, 1980.

www.ingramcontent.com/pod-product-compliance
Lightning Source LLC
Chambersburg PA
CBHW021624270326
41931CB00008B/851